HOW TO REACH THE TOP AS A
Competition Driver

Other books by Stuart Turner

THE PUBLIC SPEAKER'S BIBLE (Thorsons)
HOW TO GET SPONSORSHIP (Kogan Page)

Patrick Stephens Limited, a member of the Haynes Publishing Group P.L.C., has published authoritative, quality books for enthusiasts for more than 20 years. During that time the company has established a reputation as one of the world's leading publishers of books on aviation, maritime, military, model-making, motor cycling, motoring, motor racing, railway and railway modelling subjects. Readers or authors with suggestions for books they would like to see published are invited to write to: The Editorial Director, Patrick Stephens Limited, Sparkford, Nr Yeovil, Somerset BA22 7JJ.

HOW TO REACH THE TOP AS A
Competition Driver

Stuart Turner
& John Taylor

Foreword by
Carlos Sainz
World Rally Champion

Patrick Stephens Limited

First published in 1991

British Library Cataloguing in Publication Data
Turner, Stuart
How to reach the top as a competition driver.
1. Racing cars. Racing
I. Title II. Taylor, John
796.72

ISBN 1-85260-378-X

Patrick Stephens Limited is a member of the
Haynes Publising Group P.L.C.,
Sparkford, Nr Yeovil, Somerset BA22 7JJ.

Printed in Great Britain

1 3 5 7 9 10 8 6 4 2

Contents

Foreword

Racing and rallying are two of the most challenging and exciting sports in the world, but motorsport is expensive and the path to the top is not as easy or as clear cut as in many other sports. I was fortunate enough to have the advice and friendship of both Stuart Turner and John Taylor as I was making my way in rallying and I will always be grateful to them.

I am pleased that their advice is now available to other enthusiasts through this book. Remembering my own efforts in Formula Ford and other races before I moved into rallying, I am sure that it will be equally valuable to both race and rally drivers hoping to reach the top.

CARLOS SAINZ
WORLD RALLY CHAMPION

Introduction

Whether you take your motorsport seriously or participate just for fun, it is an expensive activity so it makes sense to do all you can to get the most out of your outlay. Too many people start motorsport without thinking things through and preparing properly, hence the heavy emphasis throughout the book on planning. As with many other activities, the key is *application* because you must have the right mental and physical approach for such a demanding sport. Nowadays you need to be more than just quick if you are to reach the top, which is why this book covers such things as finding sponsorship and marketing yourself, which you will need to do if you are to be a complete race or rally driver. It is no good clutching your leather helmet and moaning that such things weren't necessary in the good old days: motorsport is now part of showbusiness, and if you can't accept that then kindly leave the stage.

Throughout the book, for 'he' read 'she' as the advice is the same for both sexes; in fact women may actually find it easier to get sponsorship as they are still something of a minority in the sport. While the book is aimed principally at racing and rally drivers, the advice it contains could apply equally to many other branches of motorsport; it is based on many years of experience and tries to reflect the best practices. However, if you find that you have a quirky, divine talent then don't let us neuter that natural ability. We hope lesser mortals will find an amble through the pages worthwhile. We are indebted to Colin Taylor for the majority of the photographs.

A final and, we hope, not forlorn hope. Please keep in mind that while a certain amount of gamesmanship, psyching the opposition and so on may be all part of the business, going further than this and indulging in wanton bad driving can be dangerous, and can kill. Remember it is supposed to be a *sport*.

STUART TURNER AND JOHN TAYLOR

1

Self-analysis

Before you set off for racing schools or rally special stages, it is important that you do some planning. Start with some self-analysis. The experience may not be pleasant but it may save you money. For a start: how *old* are you? How far you are likely to progress in motorsport may be governed by this because stars are getting younger and, frankly, if you are in your mid-twenties and not at least part way up the ladder than forget about reaching the top.

Now what about your *mental* condition? Look in a mirror. Do you really, really believe you are a winner? Do you burn to win? How ambitious are you? How motivated are you? Are you ready to bleed in order to reach the top? It won't be easy because no one owes you a living from the sport and certainly no one owes you sponsorship. If you have an expensive hi-fi and are not prepared to sell it to fund your motorsport . . . are you sure you are really serious?

You may find the driver appraisal form set by a psychologist in Appendix A (p. 195) of interest; a sample set of answers is shown on p. 196. (Don't cheat.) Such questionnaires are by no means infallible and while they can help to give people an idea of whether they are able to cope, they will not reveal whether they have the blinding talent necessary to reach the very top. However, they do provide a broadbrush assessment and as an example of the effectiveness of such tests, when we were running one Find-a-Driver scheme across Europe we had to reduce the 'pass' mark on the form for one country (which had better remain nameless) in order to find enough people to test. It may have been coincidence (although we doubt it) but the driving standards for that particular country were lower than everywhere else. As a further example, we have collected the forms from a group of people, sealed them

Above and right *Motorsport is glamorous and exciting and the rewards at the top can be high, which is why so many people will be competing with you to reach the top.*

in an envelope, assessed the people in rally cars, and only *then* marked their forms. The quickest drivers had the best scores. Coincidence? Again, we doubt it. Anyway, however sceptical you are, why not have a try at the form?

You might even read books on psychology and stress control. Consistently, when the authors have worked with top drivers over the years, we have been staggered at the way they can regularly break lap records or special stage times then stop and quite calmly and rationally discuss what happened several laps or stages ago, and on which particular corner and under what conditions. You won't learn such control from books, which are often written for the business world (although motorsport *is* a business) and may seem somewhat cranky; but the more you understand yourself, what motivates you, what makes you tick, whether you are a loner, how well you get on with people, what are your strengths and weaknesses, and so on, the more you will be able to cope with a motorsport career. And if you feel like having your dreams or handwriting analysed to increase your self-awareness, then go ahead. Just be cautious whom you tell, because some team managers may feel you are verging on crankiness.

The more you are 'aware' of yourself the more you will be able to handle stress. You will find plenty of this as you move up through the sport, although stress in itself is not necessarily a bad

thing. The signs of stress are fairly well known: tenseness, impatience, frustration (mental as much as sexual), and the feeling that you have a lot on your mind and can't relax. The results may be the butterfly stomach, the pounding heart, the sweaty palms, and the dry mouth; but don't get alarmed because the changes are simply your body's instinctive reaction, priming you for self-survival.

Some stress is essential because it keeps you on your toes and out of danger—for instance, if you walk at night through an area known to be dangerous and you aren't alert, then you are a fool. However, if the stress gets out of hand and you keep reacting to things from which you can't escape (and who hasn't felt like blowing up in traffic jams?), then the frequent surges in blood pressure can lead to a heart attack or other problems. However, being aware of the problem can help you to combat it: if you sense you are about to get out of your car and berate a nun for pinching a parking space you had your eye on, then be sensible enough to recognize that such behaviour is irrational (if you can't see this, then you really have got behavioural problems!) and try to relax. Breathing exercises may help.

Stress control won't always work and it isn't always desirable that it should—note how athletes fidget with their necklaces and vests before a race . . . and then explode off the blocks. One of the authors makes around fifty speeches a year, and the palms sweat nearly every time: the speeches are less successful when they *don't* sweat because the speaker isn't keyed up enough to perform well.

Incidentally, if you get to the top and have the glory of an exciting and lavish life, *don't* then bleat about the pressure (as too many top sportsmen do). If you can't stand the heat . . .

As part of your self-analysis, it is worth having some idea of your IQ level. You don't have to be an Einstein to win in motorsport (rumour has it that the MENSA group in rallycross meets in a phone booth) but it is worth knowing just how bright you really are as opposed to how bright you *think* you are. Be encouraged if tests indicate that you are good at logic because a clear-minded approach to problems can play a major part in success in motorsport. Plenty of people have the physical skill, not all have the mental ability to maximize that skill.

Can you trace other winners in the family, not necessarily in motorsport? Find-a-Driver schemes, which test young drivers, often show that the most promising youngsters have mothers, fathers, brothers, or sisters with some degree of success even in totally unrelated activities like chess and tiddlywinks. This could be *genetic,* although it would perhaps need Orwellian experiments to prove it; the case may be considered proven when a famous racing driver's son wins a Grand Prix. We say 'may' be proven, not necessarily conclusively because much though sons of famous fathers may protest about the problems they have, they do tend to find doors open more easily for them, thus helping them up the ladder.

The link between successes among relatives could just as likely be *environmental* because the kids were brought up in a competitive atmosphere, be it the urge to win at budgerigar breeding or whatever. If it applies to you, just be thankful.

Last thing on your mental checklist: have you got the 'bottle'? We are not suggesting that courage and bravery are essential qualities—we hope the book makes it clear that skill is far more important. In fact, bravery *without* the necessary skill becomes a highly dangerous combination. Nevertheless it is something of a macho sport (which is why Silverstone will be under water from global warming before a woman wins a Grand Prix) and if you are not naturally a confident, even somewhat assertive character, then you may find it all rather a trial.

Having done a mental self-analysis, now consider the physical side. We don't want to be rude but . . . what shape are you? If you are very tall or very fat then you may have problems fitting in some racing cars. Being very tall is much the worse handicap (just as policemen are getting younger, race stars seem to be getting smaller). Have you got big feet? Things may be a bit cramped around the pedal area in some cars.

Incidentally, if you are disabled this need not stop you enjoying

Although some people hate to see the waste, scenes like this are a regular part of the sport. Circuit owner Tom Wheatcroft is seen on the left.

motorsport although certain conditions may prevent you getting a licence and, being realistic, others may prevent you reaching the very top ranks. Policies towards the disabled may vary between countries. In the UK for instance, various means of helping disabled drivers to compete are being mooted. The aim is that only the most seriously disabled people will need to be barred from all forms of motorsport, while those with lesser disabilities might be issued with licences restricting them to one or more particular types of motorsport.

How heavy are you? If you are overweight, are you prepared to diet? It is unreasonable to expect mechanics to toil to shave weight off a car if you carry an excess of it around your waist. If you need to lose weight, go on a *sensible* diet; keep in mind you will lose weight during an event due to dehydration, so don't starve yourself in the days leading up to a race or rally. Conversely, it may be wise not to overeat just before an event because this may dull your reactions and, on a sombre note, could make things more difficult for surgeons if you have an accident. (As an aside, find time to learn a little first aid—see Appendix B, p. 197.) During your time in motorsport, be sensible about what you eat. It's all a question of balance, and we are not advocating that you should have special health foods available at every pitstop or rally service point. Mind you, if the stuff makes you *think* you drive better . . .

Do you drink? Well, events *have* been won by people who were quite fond of their pint of real ale, but if you drink to excess then logic suggests that you will not be performing at your best. Nor will you if you smoke. Research shows that smoking can cause vision to become fuzzy and, in addition, can cause an accumulation of carbon monoxide in the bloodstream, which can impair night vision (which you will need at Le Mans and occasionally on rallies). As with drinking, if you smoke then you are likely to be that less effective than the driver who doesn't and, apart from all that, you may be even less attractive at meetings with potential sponsors if you smoke.

It's worth having a medical checkup at least once a year; you will need one before you start anyway; this will throw up your blood group which you will need to know. If you need medications of any sort, be aware of what they are for, why you need them, and what effect, if any, they are likely to have on you as a driver. Make sure your support team have the information too.

A few other points on the medical side:

- How good is your hearing? Worth knowing because the noise of engines over the years is likely to make you slightly deaf, although we suspect you won't have much joy suing engine builders for your adversity.
- Don't take drugs to try to enhance your performance.
- We considered earlier whether you have the balls for motorsport. If you have, it is worth performing a testicular self-examination every month or so because although testicular cancer is rarer than many other forms, it is most commonly found in men aged 15 to 40, which is a key motorsport age group. If the cancer is present it is usually curable, especially when detected early, so ask your doctor for advice on how to do the test.

How good is your eyesight? To get a licence, normal binocular vision is required with full visual fields, normal eye movements, and normal stereoscopic vision. You should have normal colour vision and the vision in each eye must be at least 6/9 either before or after correction. If glasses are worn the uncorrected vision as well as the corrected vision must be stated on the medical certificate.

Contact lenses may be permitted, providing there is reasonable vision in both eyes *without* the contact lenses in place. The wearing of contact lenses can only be considered when they have been worn for a period of longer than 12 months and if they are worn for a significant period each day. They should also be certified as satisfactory for motorsport by an optician.

You *can* win in motorsport wearing glasses, but apart from the mild inconvenience there may be with misting up and getting scratched (which could affect your speed), you may also have a problem convincing people that you can be a top driver because the typical picture of a driver isn't someone wearing glasses. (Incidentally, it is worth getting an optician to check whether you have reasonable night vision if you are planning to do any serious driving at night because not everybody is blessed with good vision in darkness. And if you are driving at night, don't use night driving glasses because they are of no benefit. However, if you are on events where you are likely to encounter bright lights—such as in floodlit service areas on rallies—then consider wearing dark glasses at such stops, because otherwise it may take quite a long time for your eyes to readjust.)

A checkup will have shown your medical condition, but how *fit* are you? How supple and flexible? The physical strain of motorsport can be high—you need good neck muscles, for instance, to cope with the G forces. The fitter you are the more mentally alert you will be and the more able to cope with the stress mentioned earlier. You should get into a regular routine of exercise—repetition exercises can improve concentration and, let's face it, going round and round a track may not always be the most creative of occupations. You may find a local athletics trainer intrigued at the idea of planning a programme for you. Don't go at it madheaded; remember, for instance, to warm up before starting serious exercises. The same trainer may be able to recommend a masseur to help keep you physically in trim.

A couple of other points:

- You may find it interesting to test your reactions, although don't place too much importance on the results because they can vary quite wildly. But test your own judgement by, for example, sitting in a car and asking someone 50 metres away to place two sticks at what you judge to be the width of the car, then drive forward and see how accurate you were.

- Are you homosexual? This needn't stop you reaching the top, although keep in mind that dependence on sponsorship makes teams cautious (just as it inhibits theatres from putting on experimental plays) so it may not be wise to be too overt about it.

No smoking, no drinking, careful diet, regular exercise, sell the hi-fi ... is it all starting to sound too much for you? If it is, then stop kidding yourself and accept that you haven't got what it takes to reach the top in modern motorsport.

Having conducted a thorough mental and physical stocktake, you should have an idea of what you are capable of and whether it is realistic to aim for stardom in motorsport or simply do it for fun. With this background you should then plan. Let us repeat that planning is essential. Too often people rush into race or rally programmes without proper thought, then come unstuck as a consequence. Incidentally, although we keep talking about racing and rallying, keep in mind that there are many other branches of the sport that you may choose to do just for fun, although they are unlikely to lead you to tax exile in Monte Carlo from the earnings. In your early planing don't be too hidebound. You may fancy yourself as a Formula One star, but in practice you may actually have more natural ability as a rally driver, or vice versa.

The first point in your planning is to be realistic about your finances. Work out just how much you can afford and then plan a programme accordingly, bearing in mind that it is probably better to aim to win a regional championship with a well-funded car, properly prepared and with adequate spares, than to stretch your resources too far and fail to win a national championship; you may simply end up throwing good money after bad.

An alternative, if you are a gambler, is to chance all your funding on one high visibility, make-or-break event, but you may need to face heavy disappointment if a small part on the car fails and your gamble goes with it.

When budgeting, do allow plenty for contingencies. Motorsport is expensive and however carefully you plan, you will still need funds for the unexpected.

Be realistic on funding and about your ambitions and then see if you have the self-discipline to fix some sort of tentative timetable for your career. We shall discuss this in detail later when we come to climbing the ladder, but it is reasonable at this stage to consider how many months or years you expect to spend in a particular category of the sport. Being realistic should mean being honest with your family and friends—and not least with your bank manager (whom you should try to make a friend).

Having carefully analysed your strengths and weaknesses and then considered your ambitions and financial resources, let us move on to look at what steps you should take next.

2

First Steps

Increasingly, successful drivers in mainstream motorsport have a background in karting. Maybe before long the successful ones in karting will have cut their teeth in children's pedal cycle racing (motorcycle racing produces occasional car stars so seat of the pants training is perhaps beneficial). Continuing further back along the age range, maybe pram racing will help mould youngsters' competitive instincts, and can it be long before a father insists on playing sounds of V12 engines to his unborn baby (surely no dafter than dragging a pregnant wife back to Yorkshire so that the child is then qualified to play cricket for the county)?

But if your parents were less thoughtful in their planning, what steps should you take towards a motorsport career? First, spectate

An increasing number of successful drivers come through karting and arrive in mainstream motorsport with several seasons of cut and thrust race experience.

Without officials there simply wouldn't be any racing or rallying. Marshalling will certainly put you at the heart of the action.

as often as you can afford; for rallies, your travel costs may be your only expense, while admission charges at club race meetings are unlikely to break your bank. Try to be a constructive spectator, studying different cars and different categories; keep lap charts of races and study rally results. In other words, absorb yourself in the sport. And read about it too: take one of the weekly enthusiast magazines and borrow motorsport books from the library. Not many drivers bother, but reading drivers' autobiographies can be useful because history does often repeat itself, and the struggles of one generation may be mirrored by the next.

And steep yourself in videos. The modern race and rally driver is unfortunate in that if he makes a mistake (even on the most barren corner of the remotest special stage) some smart alec will be there with a home video to film his downfall.

To further your total immersion programme, join a local motorclub—a regional section of one of the bigger national clubs may prove best because it will be closer to major motorsport than a purely parochial one. Try to get involved as a marshal (many clubs are crying out for them) and learn from the experience— although you will need to concentrate on your official duties, you should also have time to study how the good (and bad) drivers act.

If standing out in the cold on a wet rally, or being abused by a temperamental track star, hasn't cooled your ardour then it is time to start thinking about spending more on serious motorsport.

However, before you even think of buying a car, go to a race or rally school. We *strongly* recommend that you do this before, repeat *before*, you buy or hire a car with which to compete. It is

How you are likely to be assessed at a racing school.

John Watson
Performance Driving Centre
Silverstone

Silverstone Circuit · Silverstone · Nr Towcester · Northants NN12 8TN · Tel · 0327 857177 · Fax · 0327 858268 · Telex 311164 SCBRDC

ASSESSMENT FORM

Name ...... BRAD LAKE ...... Date 2/6/90 ...... Instructor ...... DEEKS ......

Approach/Attitude			Turn-in Point	A	
Familiarisation with controls	A		Line	B	
Comfort/seating position	A		Clipping Point	A	
Co-ordination/pulling away	A		Exit	B	

Gear Changing

Utilization of correct gear:

Corners	A	Suitable for further instruction: ✓
Straight	A	Introduction required:
Heel & Toe	B	Coaching Required:
Sympathy of gear change	A	
Utilization of clutch foot rest	A	

Braking Remarks:

Sufficient braking before Corner	A	
Smooth braking	A	GENERALLY VERY COMPETENT.
Braking in straight line	B	NEEDS TO GET BACK ON THE

Steering

Hand position on wheel:

Corners	B	THROTTLE SLIGHTLY EARLIER
		INTO THE CORNER TO PREVENT
Straight	A	WEIGHT TRANSFER UNBALANCING
Both hands on wheel when necessary	A	THE CAR.
Smooth turn-in	A	MAKING GOOD PROGRESS
Steering sympathy in Corner	A	THROUGHOUT, DEMONSTRATES
		GOOD POTENTIAL.

Throttle

Correct use of power	B		Above Average	A
Correct balancing of car	B		Average	B
Adherence to rev-limit	A		Below Average	C

better to find out if you have any talent using someone else's machinery (and ideally being observed by expert instructors)

A rally school appraisal form.. Note the point about not needing to declutch on FWD cars.

John Watson
Performance Driving Centre
Silverstone

Silverstone Circuit · Silverstone · Nr Towcester · Northants NN12 8TN · Tel · 0327 857177 · Fax · 0327 858268 · Telex 311164 SCBRDC

RALLY CENTRE
ASSESSMENT FORM

Name: P. JONES   Date: 28\5\90 Car: 309 GTI Instructor: LINFORD

REMARKS   Marks out of 10

STEERING TECHNIQUE REMEMBER TO WIND LOCK OFF AFTER
EXITING CORNER, MUCH BETTER ON LAST RUN   `7+`

CORRECT USE OF GEARS CLEAN SELECTION AND SYMPATHETIC
CHANGE. VERY GOOD   `9`

HEEL AND TOE   GOOD   `8`

SUFFICIENT BRAKING BEFORE CORNER GOOD JUDGEMENT BUT COULD
BRAKE A LITTLE FIRMER AND LATER   `8`

LEFT FOOT BRAKING
                                    N\A   `-`

HAND BRAKE TURN NO NEED TO DE-CLUTCH ON FRONT WHEEL
DRIVE CAR. OTHERWISE GOOD   `8`

CORRECT BALANCING OF CAR GOOD NATURAL FEEL OF CAR   `9`

CAR POSITIONING APPROACHING CORNER SOMETIMES TURNING TOO EARLY
TRY TO BE CONSISTENT.   `8`

CAR POSITIONING THROUGH CORNER MAKE MORE USE OF WIDTH
OF ROAD. MUCH BETTER ON LAST ROAD   `8`

CORRECT USE OF POWER A LITTLE TOO EARLY WITH THE POWER
ON OCCASIONS   `7+`

SUITABLE FOR MORE ADVANCED INSTRUCTION   YES/NO

COMMENTS: GOOD. IMPROVING ALL THE TIME.
DETERMINATION TO LEARN HELPS.
SUGGEST ADVANCED DAY TO START
LEARNING MORE ADVANCED TECHNIQUES
A GOOD DRIVE. WELL DONE

before you lurch out on your own. It will soon be *mandatory* to attend a racing school before being let loose on a track. And quite right too.

Don't be too rigid in your thinking at this early stage: if you can afford it, try a race *and* a rally school because you may find yourself more attracted to, or with more aptitude for, one rather than the other.

Schools vary and very much depend on the calibre of the instructors, who tend to move around; word of mouth is the best way of finding the right one. In some countries schools have formed associations committed to maintaining certain standards—look for such membership as some safeguard. Incidentally, do remember that it is in a school's interests to encourage you to take more lessons although the ethical ones won't do so if they feel you are beyond hope.

The John Watson Performance Driving Centre at Silverstone has seen more pupils than the tutors would perhaps care to count. According to the instructors, the most common faults of newcomers on the circuit are:

- A lack of finesse regarding the controls of the car—steering, bracking, and throttle. Smoothness in all of these reflects in the car being balanced and, therefore, quick.

- Turning in early. This is a very common fault, and leads to a driver having to 'read' a corner and *know* whether he has turned in at the correct point. This will become obvious as he progresses through the corner.

- Not looking ahead. Certain reference points are shown regarding cornering, but some drivers tend to look for the turning-in point, get to it, and then look for the clipping point, get to that, and then look for the exit point. The aim is to look ahead and through the corner, assess the line, and make any corrections necessary in good time.

- Braking. Most drivers do not do enough braking before a corner. This results in going in too quickly and understeering, or braking into the corner and causing acute oversteer.

- Balance. If braking before the corner is correct, drivers still tend to unbalance the car by accelerating into the corner or by not going onto a balanced throttle as they turn in. This is where the car is driven through the corner to the clipping point, not accelerating and not decelerating.

- Warming up. It is usual for some drivers to try and drive a car at its maximum in the opening lap, not allowing brakes, tyres, or themselves to warm up and become accustomed to the track.

- Too fast . . . too soon. If given a rev limit it is almost inevitable that a driver will go above this because of over confidence. This upsets the learning curve and can lead to additional problems taking more time to sort out.

- Thinking. Most drivers feel that circuit driving is just a matter of driving as on a normal road. If they know they have gone wide at a particular corner, they will continue doing this for the session, without thinking the next time around about going in slower or altering their line. They must also check the car instrumentation to log the revs on exits of corners so that they can check on their progress, and to also watch for mechanical warning instruments, taking the appropriate action where necessary.

- Self-discipline. Most drivers do not appreciate the level of self-discipline that is required. They tend to let their hearts rather than their minds rule, which will usually result in an accident, sometimes involving others as well as themselves.

Even if you don't progress from a race or rally school, you will at least have souvenirs like this to frame.

- Changing conditions. There is often a lack of respect for weather conditions. The driver can see it has started to rain on a dry track but still expects the car to behave consistently.

A formidable list which, come to think of it, doesn't just apply to newcomers. Make a note to read the points again before you go to school.

Having read all you can, and having been to a school, you should have some feel for where you want to head in the sport. Do be realistic. If school tests have shown that you are Mr Average, then take up the sport as an enjoyable, though expensive, hobby and stop dreaming about the winner's champagne and interviews on the talk shows—there is too much talent around for Mr Average to make it. Sure, you may bluff your way up one or two rungs of the ladder, but eventually your lap or stage times will find you out.

Hand in pocket time again, because if we haven't put you off and you've decided to soldier on then you will need a current *FIA Yearbook*. FIA stands for Federation Internationale de l'Automobile, which is the body that controls motorsport through a democratic process (sometimes using the term in the loosest

Often boring but always essential reading.

sense) and that delegates power to national clubs in each country (in Britain, for instance, the RAC); they in turn may authorize local clubs to run competitive events. The *FIA Yearbook*, which has been published for well over twenty years, is a big, thick, yellow-covered annual publication and is the bible for the sport because it contains all the rules and regulations for the very many and complicated international categories, as well as other useful information. It is not an easy read but you should nevertheless find time to study it, although be careful that you don't then become a barrack-room lawyer, trying to win events with the small print rather than with your driving skills. Obviously you *must* know the regulations for your event so that, for example, you can stop an assistant working on a car illegally, and because of the costs involved it is not surprising that people want their kilo of flesh if they feel they have a legitimate complaint they wish to formally protest about. But we need to remember that we are competing with many other sports for public attention: results that are announced weeks after an event because of a lengthy appeals process don't do anyone a lot of good.

As well as the yellow book, you will also need your national club's yearbook, in Britain known as the 'Blue Book' because that's the colour of the cover of the RAC MSA's (Motor Sports Association) publication; this will have not only dates of events but also *national* regulations and championship rules, plus useful names and addresses. This book also outlines what licence(s) you need. At the time of writing fees for race licences range from £23 for a Restricted to £330 for an International and for rallies from £15 to £52. These fees will (of course) rise year by year but, frankly, if they frighten you then your funding is probably too fragile for you to have much of a future in the sport anyway.

Sensibly, you can't plunge straight in at the International level. In racing, for instance, to move from a Restricted to National licence you must get Stewards' signatures (to signify a competent performance) in six Restricted or Closed races (not all at the same circuit by the way). To move from National to International 'C' you must receive signatures in three National or two National plus two Restricted, or six Restricted races (at a minimum of three different venues, thus forcing you—rightly—to gain wide experience). At this stage in your career we won't bore you with details of how you move to International 'B' then 'A', but the steps entail gaining increasing experience and success. A similar 'ladder' system operates for rally licences, too.

That's not the end of the paperwork because drivers in circuit and kart races must have a valid medical certificate approved by the national club (the blank examination report is on the licence application form), while competitors with International licences must also hold an FIA Medical Form and produce it on request. No race licence will be issued until the Medical Examination Report has been completed and signed by a registered medical practitioner. In applying for a competition licence, all drivers are required to declare any physical disability, and drivers also sign a declaration that allows the issuing body to request details of their medical history from their general practitioner. The medical examination should be carried out to a standard similar to that required for life insurance, but with specific attention to: diabetes, epilepsy, amputations, and other conditions that are felt to be incompatible with racing or rallying, although, as mentioned earlier, there is a willingness to *try* to make it possible for people to compete with these conditions.

Incidentally, people over 40 will need electrocardiograms before being granted a licence.

As you start accumulating paperwork like medical certificates and licences, establish a simple filing system, and where possible keep photostats of key documents because it will be easier to get them replaced if you lose one. Lastly on documentation, keep a detailed diary. No, not so that Alan Henry or Graham Robson can write your biography, but so that you *learn* by your experience. Log how you fared, how you found the event and the car and so on. And jot down anything that will help you do better if you do an event again.

So you've read all you can about the sport, you've spectated, you've marshalled, you've been to school, now it's time to get kitted out so that you at least start looking like a competition driver.

Apart from international racing, where FIA approved overalls must be worn, proper clothing is not actually *compulsory* in other branches of motorsport and, in theory anyway, you could rally in a lounge suit. But you'd be a bloody fool to do so. Even if you don't kit yourself out to the standards as outlined below, do please be properly protected and, for instance, never, ever, wear anything (such as a T shirt) in a material which *melts* in heat. The folly of this is, we hope, obvious.

Anyway with that in mind, buy the best equipment you can afford. It is your life you may lose if you have inadequate protection. Before you buy overalls, helmets, and so on, check with your national club for the very latest specification and buy equipment conforming to that.

Now let us consider the various items of equipment you will need and, not that it is a particularly uplifting thought, let us assume you are standing there stark naked. Any elaborate rings, bracelets, gold necklaces, or chest wigs? Remove them: they all add weight and could complicate things in an accident. Are your finger and toe nails cut to a reasonable length? They should be— not to save weight this time but because a broken finger nail can be an irritant and the space for your feet may be tight in some cars, making overlong nails painful during a long event. Stop laughing: just keep in mind that attention to detail can pay dividends.

Those goose pimples are singularly unattractive so, first get some *underwear*. Like all clothing this should be from material that satisfies the ISO 6940 test ('Textile Fabrics—Burning Behaviour—Determination of Ease of Ignition of Vertically Orientated Specimens'). An indication of this must appear on the front of the upper garment, which should extend up to and circle the neck; preferably you should have a polo neck. It's too easy to forget necks, wrists, and ankles when considering protection, but they can be very vulnerable. Incidentally, don't have underclothes too tight.

We're not sure which order you dress in, but next consider *socks*. Again the material should meet ISO 6940 and socks must be half-hose (to mid-calf).

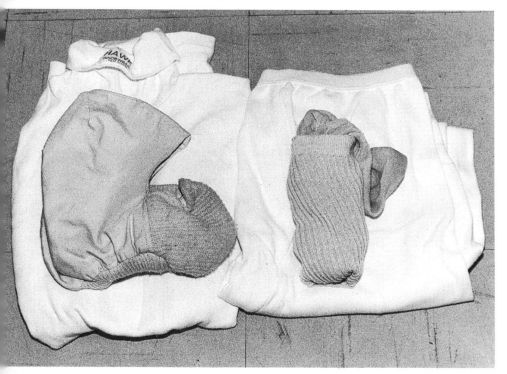

Below left and this page *Pay as much attention to what you wear under your overalls as to the overalls themselves. Costs will mount as you acquire all the equipment, but despite this don't be tempted to skimp.*

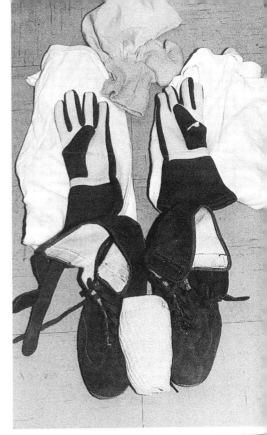

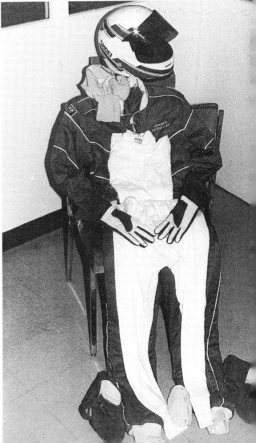

Overalls next, which should again comply with the tests and cover the whole body, extending to cover neck, wrists, and ankles. If zip-fasteners are used they must be in metal and large-toothed, mounted on flame-resistant backing tape and with a covering flap in the same material as the overall. 'Velcro'-type fasteners should be in flame-resistant material. Ankle and wrist fastenings should be situated within the sleeve or trouser so as to be covered by it in wear. Much of the phraseology here comes from the official FIA directives—isn't it comforting to know that people go to such lengths to protect you? As an example, one of the tests has to be carried out on fabric which has previously had 15 washings and 15 dry cleanings! It helps to explain why, considering the speeds and the obvious dangers, the sport is so relatively safe. But let us repeat: buy the best you can afford. Incidentally, the FIA Homologation label on drivers' overalls must be embroidered into the overall, on the back (exterior) of the collar, and include the manufacturer's name. Sewn-on printed labels will no longer be recognized from 1 January 1993.

Shoes should, in use, cover the whole foot and ankle. All interior materials should meet ISO 6940, and all fastenings or laces must be of non-fusible material. Soles must be resistant to hydrocarbons and to flames. Thread used must be flame-resistant. Shoes should be non-slip with thin soles to give you a sensitive feel, and to make them even safer do make certain that no welts can catch on any pedals, perhaps keeping you on the throttle, or off the brakes, longer than you really intended. To protect your footwear, consider a pair of slip-on overshoes to wear when out of the car if it's wet or muddy.

Materials used for *gloves* naturally must have satisfied the ISO 6940 standard, and the glove must bear a label to that effect. The back of a glove must be composed of at least two layers of material; the thread must be flame-resistant and non-melting; seam stitching must be invisible. Gloves must be fitted at the wrists, and must extend to cover the cuffs of the driver's overalls.

To complete the picture: a *balaclava*. Again, step forward the ISO 6940 test because balaclavas must comply and they must extend to enter inside the suit or undergarment all around the neck and not come free whichever way the head is moved.

Final points on clothing: when fixing badges or signs on a protective garment heat-bonding must not be used and the garment must not be cut. It is recommended that badges and signs have heat-resistant backing materials. Manufacturers should supply instructions about repairs and maintenance as well as spare heat-resistant thread.

Last, but not least, to complete the picture: a crash *helmet.*

These, bearing an approval sticker, must be worn at all times during training, practice, and competition. The user must ensure that the helmet is to a standard currently specified, that it fits properly, is secured properly, and that it is in a serviceable condition. Don't let a helmet make you feel invulnerable—total protection can never be given by any headgear, and the best of crash helmets may not entirely prevent head injury or death in a severe accident. Helmets are deliberately constructed so that the energy of a severe blow will be absorbed by the helmet and thereby partially destroy it. The damage may not be readily apparent; it is essential therefore that any helmet receiving a blow in an accident is either replaced or returned to the manufacturer for competent inspection—this of necessity must be the responsibility of the helmet user, who will have been aware of the circumstances under which the helmet was struck. Don't expect a scrutineer to spot any damage. If there is *any* doubt about a helmet's fitness, then the chief scrutineer is empowered to remove the approval sticker and impound the helmet for the event. It is the competitor himself who must ensure that the helmet he uses is fully fit for its purpose and bears an approval sticker.

You should *always* have the best possible helmet and for this reason we are NOT quoting the standards helmets must meet because books stay around for years and we don't want you to use out-of-date information—check with your national club what the latest criteria are before buying. And when buying, follow these guidelines, quoted from the *RAC Yearbook*:

To ensure satisfactory fit and security of your helmet, proceed as follows:

1. Obtain correct size by measuring the crown of your head.

2. Check that there is no side-to-side movement; a helmet should be as closely fitting as possible consistent with comfort.

3. Tighten straps securely—the chin strap must be under tension at all times; ensure therefore that the strap cannot slip. Chin cups are prohibited.

4. With head forward attempt to pull up the back of the helmet, to ensure the helmet *cannot* be removed in this way.

5. Ensure you can see clearly over each shoulder.

6. Make sure nothing impedes your breathing in the helmet and never cover your nose or mouth other than with a fire resistant balaclava or face mask. Helmets with life-support attachments must only be worn if they are connected to a life-support system.

7. Never wear a scarf, tie or other loose clothing which could come loose and possibly cause an accident.

8. Ensure that the visor can be opened with one gloved hand. (Goggles or a visor must be worn at all times during practice and competing, unless in a closed car.)

9. Satisfy yourself that the back of the helmet provides protection for your neck.

10. Do not buy from mail order unless you can satisfactorily carry out the above checks; return a helmet unused if it does not fit.

Rather a lot on crash helmets we know, but they are perhaps the most important items of equipment. So here are a few other points to keep in mind about your helmet:

- Look after it carefully, storing it in a cool, dry place away from sunlight, but don't become too attached to it—replace it every year or so.

- Don't alter the structure. If you fit an intercom system you *must* follow the helmet maker's instructions—don't just attack it with a drill.

- Only use a weak solution of soap and water to clean the helmet, and don't get the inside too wet.

- On rallies, don't let helmets roll around loose in the back of the car.

Finally on helmets, keep in mind that although some moulded plastic helmets meet approved standards, they can be badly damaged by substances such as petrol, paint, adhesives, and stickers. CARE! Such damage may not always be obvious, but if the helmet shows crazing or obvious dulling of the surface finish, then it's probably time to say farewell to it.

All that equipment will have set you back quite a lot of money so your next investment should be a strong bag to carry it all around in. It is worth keeping a record of when you bought the equipment, what cleaning it has had, and so on. Don't become over-attached to an item: renew when necessary, possibly keeping worn (but *safe*) equipment for occasions when you aren't on show for your sponsors. And talking of sponsors, put their patches on your clothing as well as your name in the appropriate positions (remembering the above cautions about abusing flame-resistant material).

3

Finding a Car

We've put it off as long as we can, but having got your licence, crash helmet, overalls, and so on, you're going to have to find a car before you can compete. Your self-analysis and attendance at race or rally schools should have pointed you towards a particular class or category, and hence which type of car you are interested in, although you may find it worthwhile finishing this book—in particular the chapter on climbing the ladder—before rushing off to beg, buy, borrow, or hire something.

If you are aiming for single-seater racing, then your main consideration will be the condition of a car and its suitability for the racing you plan. On the other hand, if you aim to use a saloon car in top flight rallying and (in some countries) racing, then you need another piece of documentation—an *homologation form* for the car you have in mind. This is an official certification by the FIA that a model of a specific car has been made in sufficient series production numbers (of which, for instance, bodywork must be identical except for a sun roof) to be classified under the regulations. An homologation application must be made by a manufacturer to FISA (the sporting arm of the FIA) through the national club of a country in which he has an assembly plant.

Each year FISA draw up a schedule for homologation procedures and, under it, copies of the forms for a car must be sent to key national clubs as well as to all members of the Manufacturers Commission, which is the forum for the works teams involved in sport. In theory, and sometimes in practice, this introduces an element of self-policing, although the 'people in glass houses' syndrome also operates. Physical checks are conducted on cars and documentation to verify production quantities.

The minimum production quantity (for instance 2500 for Groups A and N from 1 January 93, 5000 until then) must be

FEDERATION INTERNATIONALE
DU SPORT AUTOMOBILE

Homologation N°

A - 5 3 2 3

Groupe
Group **A/B**

FICHE D'HOMOLOGATION CONFORME A L'ANNEXE J DU CODE SPORTIF INTERNATIONAL
HOMOLOGATION FORM IN ACCORDANCE WITH APPENDIX J OF THE INTERNATIONAL SPORTING CODE

Homologation valable à partir du **- 1 JAN. 1987**   en groupe   **A**
Homologation valid as from _____ in group

Photo A   Photo B

R.M.C
MOTOR SPORTS
ASSN. LTD.

1. DEFINITIONS / DEFINITIONS

101. Contructeur
Manufacturer _____ FORD

102. Dénomination(s) commerciale(s) — Modèle et type
Commercial name(s) — Type and model _____ SIERRA RS COSWORTH

103. Cylindrée totale
Cylinder capacity _____ 1993.9 x 1.4 = 2791.46 _____ cm³

104. Mode de construction
Type of car construction

☐ séparée, matériau du châssis
   separate, material of chassis _____

☒ monocoque
   unitary construction   Steel sheet with composite
                            plastic body mouldings

105. Nombre de volumes
Number of volumes _____ 3

103. Nombre de places
Number of places _____ 5

F.I.S.A.

1

The homologation form is virtually the birth certificate for a production car in motorsport. The perforations are to stop forgeries.

reached within twelve consecutive months and, *note carefully,* homologation lapses five years after annual production has fallen below 10 per cent of the production minimum of the group in question—so if a manufacturer just does a special one-off run for homologation, then the model will be ineligible after five years.

An homologation form is in effect the 'birth certificate' of a car and includes measurements and photographs of all aspects so that scrutineers (and sometimes rivals) can check that a vehicle complies with the rules. Forms have to be in the language of the

Lists of options like this on an homologation form are a reasonable indication that the manufacturer takes motorsport seriously.

		N° Ext. _____
Page ou ext. Page or ext.	Art. Art.	Description Description
7	605	Reinforced rear cover for rear axle case Photo 90 - 11
7	605	Strengthened front axle case, interchangeable with standard unit Photo 90 - 12
7	605	Heavy duty front axle case, Mounted in same position as standard unit and incorporating heavy duty gears, bearings and shaft assemblies type FF1/A Photo 90 - 13 type FF1/B Photo 90 - 14
7	605	Support stays for heavy duty front axle assembly Photo 90 - 15
6	603	Final drive reduction gear (built into Gearbox) Ratio 1.800 : 1.714 : 1.619 : 1.545 : 1.478 : Teeth 36/20 : 36/21 : 34/21 : 34/22 : 34/23 :
7	605	Alternative final drive ratios (heavy duty rear axle assembly) (9" unit) Ratio 5.11 : 4.89 : 4.67 : 4.44 : 4.27 Teeth 46/9 : 44/9 : 42/9 : 40/9 : 47/11 Ratio 4.09 : 3.82 : 3.64 : 3.42 : 3.25 Teeth 45/11 : 42/11 : 40/11 : 41/12 : 39/12 Ratio 3.08 Teeth 37/12
7	605	Alternative final drive ratios (Strengthened axle assembly) (7/7.5" units) Ratio 5.11 : 4.57 : 4.44 : 4.43 : 4.12 : Teeth 46/9 : 32/7 : 40/9 : 31/7 : 33/8 : Ratio 3.86 : 3.625 : 3.375 : 3.14 Teeth 27/7 : 29/8 : 27/8 : 22/7

country of origin but—no doubt to your relief if you are planning to compete with a foreign car—French or English translations must be supplied. Dimensions, incidentally, are metric apart from wheel measurements.

Manufacturers don't always use just one supplier for a component so 'supply variants' are allowed to cover this, while 'option variants' cover items that are additional to, or replace, those on the basic model and are available on request (which is

Endless details like these on an homologation form mean that scrutineers can readily check a car for eligibility.

FEDERATION INTERNATIONALE DU SPORT AUTOMOBILE

Homologation N° **A-5323**

Groupe
Group **A/B**

| Marque Make | FORD | Modèle Model | SIERRA RS COSWORTH |

Dimensions intérieures comme définies par le Règlement d'Homologation
Interior dimensions as definied by the Homologation Regulations.

B	(Hauteur sur sièges avant) (Height above front seats)	1060 mm
C	(Largeur aux sièges avant) (Width at front seats)	1270 mm
D	(Hauteur sur sièges arrière) (Height above rear seats)	970 mm
E	(Largeur aux sièges arrière) (Width at rear seats)	1360 mm
F	(Volant — Pédale de frein) (Steering wheel — brake pedal)	630 mm
G	(Volant — paroi de séparation arrière) (Steering wheel — rear bulkhead)	1630 mm
H	= F+G =	2260 mm

RAC MOTOR SPORTS ASSN. LTD.

where manufacturers' creativity can play a part—and where you can see whether a company takes its sport seriously). Add pages for erratum and it's not surprising that an homologation form can run to well over 100 pages. And you thought motorsport was only about pressing down the right foot? Such innocence.

Finally, remember to check the creativity of the 'variants' as an indication of whether the manufacturer is serious about people using the vehicle in motorsport, and don't forget to check when the car falls out of homologation because this could have a major effect on its value.

What is the spares situation for any vehicle you are thinking of getting? Ask drivers running the same model. And what is the cost of key items? Regular renewal will be an essential part of your programme and therefore a key element in your budget.

When your research into such things has given you a rough idea of the sort of car you want, you then have to decide whether to hire or buy.

Clearly *hiring* is simplest, particularly if the deal involves on the ground support. You then simply turn up, perform elegantly, and drive away afterwards clutching your trophy; someone else puts the car onto the transporter and drives it away.

Word of mouth is perhaps as good a way as any of finding a car to hire; the race and rally schools should be able to give you a lead, as should preparation companies.

When you find a suitable car to hire, set out in writing exactly what you are getting, what backup support, what the situation is over insurance cover, what happens if it blows up, etc, etc. Both authors have been privileged to work with top drivers with no legal contracts, just handshakes; hiring a car is most definitely *not* an area for such a relaxed approach, which is why a typical hiring contract is given in Appendix C (p. 199). Sod's Law says that if you don't have a clear understanding and put it in writing, something will go wrong that could lead to litigation. For the same reason you should be very, very careful about borrowing cars from friends. If you do, even if it's from your blood-brother, put things in writing.

When hiring, by the way, having laid down what *you* should be getting, do accept that the people hiring the vehicle should be getting something too, namely a profit. Unlike many other sports, motorsport *is* expensive, often horrendously so, and if hire quotes cause you apoplexy . . . isn't it time to consider another sport?

If you decide to *buy* a car you need to decide whether you want, or can afford, new or second-hand, and whether you want a ready-prepared car or something needing work. If the latter, are you going to do it yourself or have it done for you? The plus points of self-preparation are that you will be totally familiar with your car and you should save on labour costs; the downside is the time and sheer effort it may take, to say nothing of the bruised and cut fingers, while you may also have a steep learning curve to climb if it's an unfamiliar vehicle.

If you do decide to buy (we're sorry to keep labouring the point), do have a realistic budget and sensible aims in mind. If your budget will not stretch to the sort of car you would really like, you may consider a joint venture with a friend; but the same caveats apply to this as to hiring a car: *put things in writing.*

If you are considering buying a rally car, a key decision is whether to have left- or right-hand drive. If you really want to get anywhere you *must* go for left-hand drive because the vast majority of works teams operate such machines. Drivers who operate in both left- and right-hand drive cars maintain it is possible to switch quite quickly once you are used to it, although there is a case for arguing that if you are going to rally left-hand drive you should use a left-hand drive vehicle as a normal road car, so that changing gear with your right hand really does become second nature.

Finding a car? If you want a second-hand one study the enthusiast magazines, go to races and rallies, and generally ask around. Race and rally schools may know of suitable cars for sale, as may the preparation shops, while very occasionally there are auctions of competition cars. Even if you are mechanically knowledgeable, it is still worth taking a friend with you when viewing a car in order to get a second opinion.

Above all, *don't get carried away.* Don't be seduced into thinking a particular car is the only possible one for you; there'll be another one coming along behind. And if a car is advertised or alleged to have a great competition history, calm down: while 'winner of this or that' may add value at a classic car auction in the long term, in the short term it probably just means that it is ready for major surgery.

Consider if the car will let you show just how good you are: are other people competing with similar machinery for instance? If you run a weird one-off, the commentators and crowd may love you for adding variety, and you will certainly get noticed; *but* team managers who may be able to give your career a boost may not be able to tell just how good you are or whether the success is due to you or your car; if you beat an established star in exactly the same car, then you will leave no one in any doubt. Keep in mind, too, that the spares and homologation situation may be more difficult with oddball cars.

It goes without saying, but nevertheless we had better say it,

Keep calm when buying a competition car. There will invariably be another one.

that all the warnings about buying any form of second-hand road car apply equally to motorsport machinery. Before you buy or hire a car draw up a checklist, which should include at least the following points, plus anything specially relevant to your particular category:

1. Is the car damage free? If not, can it be safely and readily repaired? What will be the likely cost of any repairs? Even if it appears damage free, still look very carefully for old repairs and judge if these have been professionally done. Remember

that a poorly repaired shell will usually result in a poorly handling car.

2. Is there any sign that a proper maintenance log has been kept?

3. Does the workshop in which it is housed look reasonably tidy, and does the owner (or his mechanic) appear to know what he has been about?

4. Are the safety devices adequate? Carefully inspect the roll cage, seat belts, seats (and their mounting points), and fire extinguishers.

5. If it's a saloon, then the hardest used and most abused component will be the bodyshell. Careful inspection is essential.

6. If the vehicle in question has a fuel cell fitted, make sure the manufacture date is visible and check that the cell is within the specified age limit.

7. Check the condition of the brakes and steering components.

8. Note how quickly the oil light goes out when starting the engine. Does the oil pressure drop dramatically when warm? If it does, then this is a sign of a tired engine; a rebuild could be costly. Check the engine number and ask who rebuilt it last, then ring that engine builder and verify the information. Check the validity of other repair bills, invoice dates, and so on.

9. Road or track test the vehicle and assess the handling, making *very* sure you are adequately insured. Check the engine, gearbox, and axle for noise and note the efficiency and balance of the brakes.

10. If in doubt, get a second or third opinion.

11. Don't get carried away. Remember your planning, remember your budgets . . . are you *sure* it is the right car for you? If so, go ahead with a final precaution—be sure you and the vendor understand exactly what you are buying. You wouldn't want to come back and find worn tyres have replaced good ones or that expensive parts have gone missing, would you?

Finally, the vendor will no doubt want to be sure your money is good, so he won't be able to complain if you in turn check that the car is actually his to sell.

4

Car Basics

Now you have a car. But before you attack it with a spanner, let us have a short interlude to consider what happens to a car during a race or rally; how and why a car behaves like it does. You may feel that with your natural talent you don't really need to know too much about the theory. Agreed, it is possible to become a top driver purely on instinct (several have done so); but nowadays, with sophisticated technology, the more you understand, the more you will be able to communicate with engineers, tyre technicians, and so on. Such communication will give you that extra fraction of a percent, that all-important fraction that produces winners. With one warning: talented engineers can be prima donnas with very firm opinions and may not welcome drivers constantly sounding off with half-baked ideas. As a driver, learn to assess engineers' strengths (and weaknesses, though the great ones may not admit to any) and learn to work *with* them, giving them the essential feedback they need if a car is to be improved.

If you are to communicate with engineers you need to understand some of the technical terms used. For instance:

Camber angle is the inclination of the tyre when you look at the car from the front. If the top of the tyre leans inwards, you have negative camber; if it leans outwards you have, not surprisingly, positive camber. If you consider how a car may roll, you will see why negative camber will keep more rubber on the road under hard cornering.

Castor angle. Castor is what provides the self-centring effect to steering and, really, makes a car driveable. From the side of the car, positive castor is the amount the kingpins incline rearwards. We won't consider any forward inclination (providing negative castor) because that produces no self-centring action and is usually only found on earth-moving equipment. Your rally car may inadvertently move earth during your formative years of course, but that's a different matter.

Bump steer. One of the most critical factors affecting vehicle handling and steering is the wheel alignment. It is important to set the tracking of the front and rear wheels to the recommended values (usually 1, 2, or 3 millimetres of 'toe-in'—see later) but it is also vital to have a knowledge of what happens to the wheel alignment as the wheels move up and down. This is known as the kinematic steer, or more usually bump steer.

The bump steer can be measured by the following method:

- Remove the road springs and bump rubbers.
- Refit the dampers in the case of a McPherson strut.
- Put the wheels to be measured on turntables or a greased plate.
- Fit wheel alignment measuring equipment.
- Lower the car fully on a jack.
- Measure the ride height at the wheels left and right.
- Record the toe-in between both wheels and record the ride height measurement.
- Raise the car on the jack in increments of 10mm, checking that it is equal left and right and record the ride heights and toe-in for each position.
- Repeat measurements until full rebound, and for accuracy lower the car gradually repeating the measurements.

When measurements have been completed the values are plotted on a graph of toe-in against wheel travel. The resulting curve is known as the bump steer curve.

The first requirement for good handling is for the bump steer curve to be near to vertical, with only small deviations of toe-in as the wheel moves up and down. A 'small deviation' is of the order of 2 min angle per 10mm travel per wheel.

Measured as both wheels together this would be 4'/cm. Thus, over a wheel travel of say 60mm bump and 60mm rebound (12cm total) a total change of track of 48' could be recorded (⁴/₅ of a degree).

The suspension designer will decide from experience what bump steer curve he is trying to achieve to give good handling. This is an immensely complex subject since the characteristic on small angles of lock, as well as characteristic in the straight ahead condition, has to be considered.

A useful rule of thumb would be:

Front Axle	Static toe-in:	20 min or about 2mm
	Compression (bump):	2 min/cm toe-out
	Rebound:	2 min/cm toe-in
Rear Axle	Static toe-in:	20 min
	Compression (bump):	2 min/cm toe-in
	Rebound:	2 min/cm toe-in

On the front axle the bump steer can be modified by various means:

1. By adjusting the castor angle;
2. By shimming the steering rack up or down;
3. By changing the relationship between the steering rack length and the track rod length in comparison to the wishbone length;
4. By moving the steering arm up or down.

The *spring rate* is the force exerted by the spring for a particular deflection, or change in length. The spring rate is measured in:

Metric units:	N/mm
	Kg force/mm
	Kp/mm
Imperial units:	16 force/in

A typical linear spring rate for the front suspension of a rally car might be

$$500 \text{ lb/in}$$

The conversion factor is 1 N/mm = 5.595 lb/in

$$\frac{500}{5.595} = 89.4 \text{ N/mm}$$

Some springs are designed to have a progressive characteristic. This means that the rate changes through the range of travel of the spring. Thus typically the rate of a progressive spring may be quoted as 63-76-109 N/mm to describe its change in characteristic through the range. Also quoted is the 'spring rate at the wheel' which is efective rate calculated through the ratio of the wheel travel to the spring travel and including the lever ratio.

Damper rates. Shock absorbers apply a force in relation to the *speed* at which the shock absorber or road wheel is travelling. The force is therefore independent of the stroke or wheel travel. Shock absorbers need to be able to react to all conceivable input speeds with the desired reactive force. The characteristic of these forces is defined by the valving and porting within the units, and is usually designed to give different values in the compression and rebound directions.

The damper rates are normally presented by the manufacturer in the form of a chart, from which the forces can be read off for any velocity.

To give a feel for the velocities involved,

1. A mild undulation in the road would be 0.2 m/sec damper velocity.
2. If the road wheel hits a brick the damper velocity would be about 2 m/sec.

Suppliers have their own conventions for describing rates. Bilstein for example tests all of its units at a velocity of 0.52 m/s.

A typical description would be 350/150, implying:

> Rebound force of 350 kp (3500N) at 0.52 m
> Compression force of 150 kp (1500N) at 0.52 m/s

Toe-in is the angle by which wheels tend to come together at their front edge; toe-*out* is the reverse. Either toe-in or -out is designed to induce the wheels to run parallel when the car is on the move and all the tolerances in the system have been taken up. If you set a car up to be 'perfect' when static, it won't be so when on the move—a car is never so stable or docile as when it is standing still; it is when you put it into motion that it can become an animal.

The moment you move a car forward under acceleration you introduce forces that will cause the front of the car to lift and the rear of the car to squat. The opposite applies under braking when the front will squat and the back will lift. And you introduce further, different, forces when cornering, which is why there is so much loose talk about *oversteer* and *understeer.*

All standard cars have a built-in characteristic, which is understeer. In other words, when you turn the steering wheel the car will try to go straight on rather than round the corner in the direction you want to go; it tries to steer a much wider arc. With oversteer the opposite occurs and the back of the car tries to step out of line; if the corner goes to the right, the back of the car will try to step out to the left, taking you round the corner more sharply and into a spin if you are not careful. An understeering car is better for Mr Average Motorist because it is more stable and safe—if in trouble Mr Average is likely to yank on more lock, which could become fraught in an oversteering car, leading to a spin.

Which is better for motorsport? For rallies, particularly when some of the stages are unknown, it is safer to have an oversteering car. If it is a pace note event, with every corner known, then a mildly understeering car is probably quickest; *but* if you then lose contact at high speed, perhaps through hitting ice or gravel, it is more difficult to get out of trouble because the car will be less responsive. Note how often, when ice first appears on the roads in winter, motorists usually slide into ditches on the outside of corners, on the left of right-hand bends and vice versa.

Similar principles apply to the track. Any force, whether oversteer or understeer, causes friction and friction slows a car. That is why if you watch modern rallying and racing, the cars do not get out of line but are as neutral as possible all the time with drivers feeding in appropriate power according to the severity of the corners and the state of the surfaces. Rally spectators may mourn the end of cars swinging the rear ends from side to side approaching corners but those days have gone forever. Smoothness is king. However, while being smooth you can still induce forces to give you a slight oversteer or understeer bias. If you turn into a corner with the car in a neutral state, with no power applied and on a trailing throttle, and then feed in the power, you squat the back of the car down, the front goes slightly light, and the back of the car will be trying to step out of line slightly; but if you keep your foot down and increase the power all the way through the corner, you can keep the car in a constant state of balance. A party trick at rally training days is to put a driver on a loose surface and ask him to keep a car circling a pylon purely on throttle control.

Your driving technique could be affected by the configuration of your car, but not what you are actually trying to achieve. It doesn't matter whether a car is front-wheel drive, rear-wheel drive, or four-wheel drive: you are looking for the easiest, smoothest, cleanest way round a corner without inflicting too much friction on the tyres from the road surface. The search for smoothness is just one of the reasons why so much attention must be paid to suspension and why there is likely to be so much interest in active suspension systems in the future.

If you are to be smooth in your driving, then *brakes* are also critical and you should be looking to have the best possible within the regulations, but without going over the top. It's no use having the biggest, heaviest brakes that are fitted to the factory cars of the same type as you run if you've got 100 hp less than them; if you are carrying an extra 15 kilos of brakes but the power from the engine is not enough to maximize the use of those brakes, then you may not be getting any benefit for your expenditure.

The *balance* of the brakes on a car is important. If, for example, you have all the brake bias to the front so that the front wheels are locking all the time, that is inefficient. Constantly locking the rear wheels coming into corners will be just as inefficient and the car will be trying to slide round on you, although some drivers have a slight brake bias to the rear and then use this bias to help kick the back of the car out of line to make the car oversteer, which for them is a safe attitude. As a general rule, don't stray too far from 'recognized practice' on brakes as ones that are too hot—or, just as important, too cold—don't work very well.

You can of course control how a car brakes by your application of the brake pedal (and not least by the application of your brain power) but, given that you are braking in a smooth manner—going on the brakes softly and then gradually increasing the load—then ideally you want the brakes 'tuned' so that all four wheels give the same bite, without the front or rear operating a greater force than the other.

Although it's useful to consider the various components of a car individually, they don't work in isolation on an event and one of the essential skills for a driver to cultivate is to be able to relate the various parts of a car so that they work well together.

If a car has a particular problem (let's face it, some are just dogs to drive) it may be possible to compensate for it, or at least lessen its adverse impact on performance, by re-tuning other areas. This may be quicker and more sympathetic to the car than just 'driving through' the problem, as people with raw talent sometimes do.

You must consider *all* the key elements in your car. Axle ratios, for instance, can be as, or more important than engine performance. For example, it is no use having a standard ratio on a twisty mountain road—you will never use the higher gears in the box because you will be in first, second, or third all the time.

All standard production cars have synchromesh *gearboxes*, and with saloons running in group A you can only use a dog box if the manufacturer has homologated one. If you are using the standard box (say, in Group N) the main thing to remember is to be patient with it—you may think that, everytime you change gear, the faster you are the more time you will save. Maybe, but if you continually try to beat the synchro you may eventually break it and you won't be able to get *any* gears. Goodbye laurel wreath.

A dog box is much faster provided you have the timing of the gear selection right; the engine speed and the next ratio speed must be co-ordinated as you engage the gear. It is possible to change gear with a dog box without using the clutch, but if you continually do so and your timing is bad you will break it.

For axles and gearboxes to be earning their keep you need an *engine*. We've deliberately left this near the end because if you

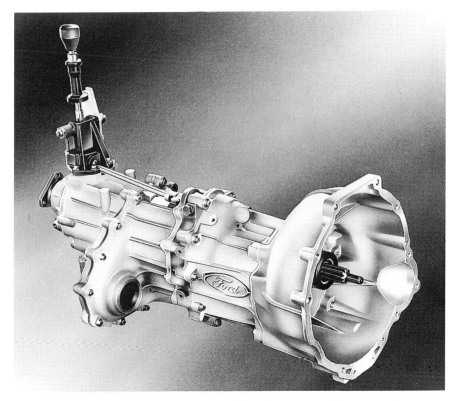

In the upper reaches of Group A, special gearboxes like this 7-speed one can cost as much as the basic car.

have poor suspension or bad brakes all the power in the world won't make you a winner. In fact it may make you dangerous, to yourself and, more importantly, to other drivers. If you've got no brakes or the suspension is trying to pitch you off the road, you can't apply power, so why bother having more of it? Too often people spend their first pounds on the engine. Wrong, wrong, wrong. Get your car handling and stopping properly first.

In your initial learning period it's not a bad idea, on rallies at least, to use a virtually standard engine (perhaps with lower gear ratios) because the manufacturer designs cars to operate in all conditions, which means that the power is delivered smoothly all the way through the power band. Just concentrate on climbing your own individual learning curve and don't get an inferiority complex as horsepower figures are bandied around in bar-room chat. Incidentally, if you are in one-make races and someone leaves you on the straight don't automatically assume he has cheated and has more horses—are you sure it isn't that he had more skill through the corner preceding the straight?

If someone boasts that they've got maybe 280 horsepower from a 2-litre normally-aspirated engine, there's a very good chance that all the power is at the top end, with nothing at 4000/4500 revs. It isn't until, say, the revs reach 7500/8000 rpm that the engine starts to earn its keep, and even then the power band may only be over 1000/1500 revs. All of which can make a car very difficult to drive.

With a turbocharged engine, when the turbocharger comes up on boost it can give a lot of sudden power, and in fact, with two-wheel drive turbocharged rally cars working in slippery conditions, the authors have known of drivers begging for *detuned* engines because they were constantly breaking traction. Once you break traction the car is in control of *you*, you aren't 100 per cent in control of *it*; and if the energy is going into spinning the wheels (overheating the tyres, by the way), the car is not driving forward and you are losing time.

So the moral with engines is to aim for *usable* power rather than maximum power. And, by the way, when people are quoting maximum horsepower figures to you, do keep in mind that some horses are extremely small and undernourished animals.

Not quite finished yet. Even if you have the right power it still has to be put on the road to be any use—which means you need

An illustration of why you need to understand tyres. From left to right this line-up of Pirelli tyres would be used for: very muddy slushy gravel; not too muddy soft gravel; dry hard gravel; full soft snow (note the studs and also how narrow the tyre is); packed ice and snow with some slush; full wet tarmac; intermediate damp tarmac; and finally, far right, dry tarmac.

Tyre warmers in use. Before an F1 race the paddock is full of banks of them, with generators buzzing away. Even on rallies their use can save vital seconds over the first part of a special stage.

tyres. If you consider that works teams will plan to have *at least one thousand tyres per car* for a Monte Carlo Rally, and then look at the number in a race paddock, you will appreciate what a major contribution to performance they can make—which is perhaps not surprising when you consider that all the control functions of a car are transmitted through them. Then consider that the areas of contact—about the size of the soles of your shoes—are in contact with the road for no more than five-thousandths of a second at a time at speed and you begin to realize what complex things they are. You can move on to the 1000-tyre lunacies later, but in your early days of rallying or racing it pays to stick with durable tyres that will last. This may mean quite a hard compound for racing tyres, which will require careful warming up, but you should be able to get quite a few races out of a set.

For rallying, if the works boys are on some exotic tyres for the special stages, comfort yourself with the thought that they may only last for 20 or 30 kilometres. Choose something more conservative that will last longer; this should mean that your budget should last longer, too. As it will if you plan the overall preparation of your car carefully, a process we shall begin in the next chapter.

5

Preparing for Preparation

Before you begin to prepare a car, pause to consider what *resources* you have. Are you going to do the work yourself or pay someone to do it for you? If you are going to do it yourself, do you have adequate knowledge? Remember, it could be dangerous if you prepare a car badly. If you haven't got the knowledge, could you work on a friend's car for a while (under supervision, of course) to get experience? Would the same friend then come and help you with your car? Should you go to night school to improve your skills? With the increased interest in motorsport, as well as in renovating classic cars, technical colleges are sometimes running courses that could help you.

How much time have you got? Will it be enough or do other hobbies compete for your time? If they do, are you *sure* you are serious about the sport? What are you doing with other hobbies if you are trying to reach the top in motorsport?

Are you fit? You will need to be fit to be a good race or rally driver, but consider too if you are physically capable of preparing a car; humping parts around can be arduous.

Having considered your physical condition, what about your mental state? Have you got the right degree of dedication to prepare a car? It is highly likely that during the process *something* will go wrong; you will need the resilience to persevere and plan your way through the problem in order to prepare the car properly. And talking of mental dedication, *planning* is one of the vital elements in successful car preparation. Are you sensible enough to sit and think through your preparation logically? Too often people tear a car to pieces . . . and then forget where everything goes. So plan.

Equipment

The first piece of 'equipment' you'll need will obviously be space in which to build a car. Cars have been built in bedrooms but the cost of then taking windows out to remove them has bust many a budget (to say nothing of the subsequent cost of divorce settlements). You really need slightly better facilities. A simple lock-up may be perfectly adequate, but do consider the following:

- Are the premises secure? If you have any choice, then side-hinged doors are better than up-and-over ones because they are less draughty and can be made more thief-proof. Any windows? If they have clear glass then either add curtains or, better still, cover the windows with stick-on plastic to make them opaque (cheaper than re-glazing). Does a window open to let air in and fumes out? At least one should.

- Is there a water supply? Any sanitation?

- Is there a telephone? An answerphone and fax machine may become useful additions.

- Do you have adequate lighting? Fluorescent strip lights are best. Don't forget you'll need one, or two, inspection lamps, which means an ample supply of power points, preferably waist high not on the floor. Is the wiring safe? If in doubt get it checked.

- Do you have heating? Working on a car in unheated premises in winter can be quite a turn-off. And for the inner man, or woman, an essential fitment will of course be a kettle, which should have an automatic cut-off. You may also consider pin ups and nude calendars to raise the temperature—if they are too tacky just remember that they may not impress more conservative sponsors. Race numbers and rally plates are of course appropriate display items, as are laurel wreaths—even if you did get them for ballroom dancing.

- Is the place clean? If not, tidy it up (emulsion paint shouldn't break the bank) and, before you bring the car in, take a moment to repair any leaks in the roof and plug up draughty gaps in the walls. And if at all possible *seal* the floor (levelling it if necessary at the same time) to stop dust and, not least, encourage an air of cleanliness. The cleaner the place, the better your preparation will be and, in addition, the more you will impress potential sponsors. To this end it's not a bad idea to get a friend to visit your premises and give you his critical first impressions; he or she may spot some eyesore to which you've become accustomed.

- Can body panels be stored in the roof space to save them getting damaged while the rest of the car is being prepared? If so, install strong hooks.
- Does the place have adequate access for vehicles?

You won't need planning if you are simply working on a car as a hobby; but, nevertheless, if you are going to be banging late at night, have you considered the effect on any neighbours? It won't help your motor racing career if you have to fight a cumbersome court case if they are trying to stop you preparing the car. If there is any doubt, visit people and tell them of your hopes and boyhood dreams.

Having sorted out the basic premises, you will now need some *equipment*. An essential will be a trolley jack together with substantial (repeat substantial) axle stands; you are going to be working under a car quite a lot so these are vital.

You will need a strong bench with a vice, plus plenty of shelves and lots of bins, clearly marked, in which to keep various components. And get into the habit of *inspecting* parts you buy, don't leave it to the last minute to find that a part is not to spec or faulty.

Seal the floor of any preparation shop to prevent dust. Note the sponsor's message designed to register when the boot is up.

Suitable stands will be invaluable when working on engines, gearboxes, axles, etc. And do have plenty of storage bins.

You will need an engine hoist. If you've got hefty rafters in the building this may be simply a strong pulley. Amongst other things, you should have a tracking gauge, camber and castor gauges, a few straight edges, and a spirit level. And, of course, you will need tools; the lesson here is to buy the best quality you can afford. Shoddy tools will not only break quickly but may break your bones in the process. A drill will be essential. Before buying spanners, study the workshop manual (if it's a production car), or build sheet, or whatever, for other cars to guide you on the sizes you need. Then vow to always use the right size. Build up a collection of tools as you need them—don't go all starry-eyed into an accessory or hardware shop because you'll probably buy far too many and they'll never get used. If you have a board to mount the tools on and then paint silhouettes of them, you'll be able to tell if anything is missing (perhaps left in the car to jam the throttle open—it has happened) and, just as important, you'll be encouraged to keep the place tidy. Mount a blackboard somewhere to make notes on.

Have some form of container for oil and radiator waste; the bottom half of an oil drum is ideal. You will need sawdust for cleaning up the floor together with a broom, bucket, and spade. If you skid on spilt oil, it may be amusing as you do an impromptu impression of Torville and Dean; it will be less so if you then break a bone. You probably won't need a welding kit, sandblasting equipment, or a compressor at this stage because you can hire them, take the parts to places with such items, or people will visit you with mobile equipment.

What you *must* have is an adequate fire extinguisher or two— and do remember that the time to read the instructions is *before* the flames start licking your ankles. As further safeguards let people know where you are, never work under a car unless it is properly supported, and be cautious in storing petrol. Be equally cautious about getting grease in any cuts. Have a first-aid kit and, incidentally, have a tetanus injection before you start your preparation work.

Although it can sound dramatically dynamic, be a shade wary of midnight oil because if you are tired you may make mistakes that could be dangerous later (or even immediately if you bash your knuckles). *Of course* last minute panics will arise from time to time, but plan to avoid such things if possible. If you are doing your own preparation and you work several all-nighters before an event, do realize that you will probably be in no fit state to perform properly. Even consider missing an event to get you and the car right for the next one.

Having considered safety, now think about the actual work you plan to do. Time spent in this way can be invaluable because if you get the preparation right you may save major breakdowns, not least in your budget.

Get into the habit of keeping records. Have a bible for the car with a record of everything you do to it. Consider photographs of key items; such a record will not only help you remember what fits where but will also be proof to future buyers that the work was done on the car. Your log should note when key parts were fitted so that you will know when they have reached their 'change by' date. Get hold of build sheets from race or rally car manufacturers or preparation shops; for production cars you should have a copy of the workshop manual. Visit your friendly preparation shop to pinch their ideas, and also to find someone you can lean on for

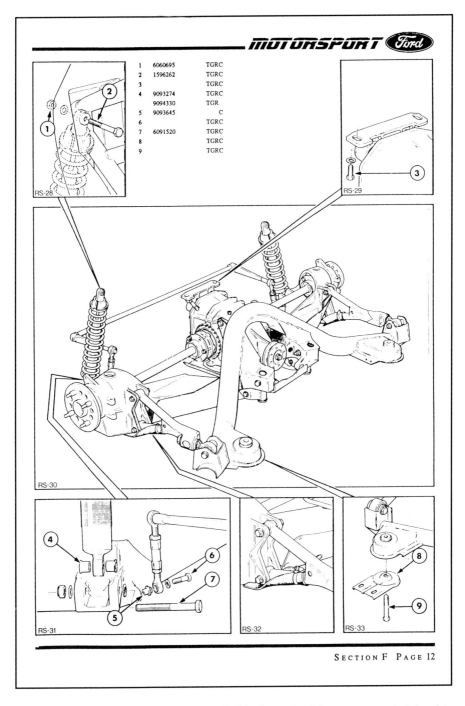

1	6060695	TGRC
2	1596262	TGRC
3		TGRC
4	9093274	TGRC
	9094330	TGR
5	9093645	C
6		TGRC
7	6091520	TGRC
8		TGRC
9		TGRC

SECTION F PAGE 12

When planning your preparation, get hold of any booklets or manuals like this for your car.

VEHICLE BUILD SPECIFICATION

EVENT RAC RALLY   DATE Nov 90

CAR P6 FIORIO , P7 AIRIKKALA , P8 WILSON .

REGISTRATION Nº

CHASSIS Nº

ENGINE Nº MOUNTUNE.

START Nº 1 P7 , 8 P8 , 12 P6 .

FOR 1ST DAY TARMAC
F 1"-14 φ φ MW/N
R ⅞"-14 φ φ CW-Y
F 180MM R 185MM.

SPECIFICATION	FRONT	REAR
SUSPENSION		
SPRINGS	54-73-109	30-35-45
DAMPERS	500/200	350/130.
BUMP RUBBERS	94x32 +6MM SPACER.	75MM +6MM SPACER.
*ANTI ROLL BAR	NONE	NONE
*BLADE POSITION	—	—
CASTOR	3½° (430mm).	—
CAMBER	−2½° (303mm)	0° (USING CAMBER) MW/A ADJUSTERS −1° 1A.
TOE IN	2MM MW/AF 4MM 1A	3MM
*RIDE HEIGHT	230MM.	220MM.
BRAKES	φ315x28 PLAIN DISC.	φ285x25 PLAIN DISC
MASTER CYLINDER	0,75"	0,7" P6,P8 , 0,625" P7.
BRAKE PAD MATERIAL	BLUE CARBON METALLIC	BLUE CARBON METALLIC .
CLUTCH	φ200MM SINGLE PLATE 6 PADDLE CERAMETALLIC SPRUNG CENTRE .	—
WHEELS	7x16, 6x16 SPEEDLINE.	7x16, 6x16 SPEEDLINE.
TYRE	215/60x16 SG90	215/60x16 SG90
COMPOUND	M7,M8 .	M7,M8
PRESSURE	1.8 BAR.	1.8 BAR.

GEARBOX SPEC. NUMBER MS90 22/34 /50/50 /60 Nm.

CENTRE DIFF. CHAIN RATIO

FRONT AXLE. LSD 7½" 65 Nm.

REAR AXLE LSD 9" 200 Nm MAG CASE.

Keep records! You must know the exact specification that your car is running in on any event.

advice. Seek out parts suppliers; get their stock lists, establish the supply situation, and, not least, their prices. You will remember to budget properly for parts, won't you?

With all that background information, list what needs doing. If it's a new vehicle or one straight from a preparation shop, then obviously it will need less than if it's a tired old banger. Put your work list in order of priority. You don't need a detailed, critical path analysis done on an expensive computer (although being computer literate will become increasingly important), but you must plan to do things in a logical order.

Do beware of the 'big strip'. It is very, very tempting to tear a car to pieces. That's the easy bit. Putting it together again when you've forgotten where everything goes is less exhilarating. If you need to strip a car down to its basic shell, take out complete assemblies and *leave them complete* until you are ready to work on a particular area. And before you take a car down, do take proper measurements so that you know the base line from which you started.

A few general points about planning for preparation:

- When preparing a car, try to do so in such a way that it will always be as easy as possible to work on—this may, for instance, mean considering captive nuts in difficult places to reach.

- Don't grumble because we've placed so much stress on planning and attention to detail. Just remember proper preparation, with care about the lengths and sizes of bolts and so on, takes no longer than bad, it is more reliable, it is safer, and it is more likely to impress scrutineers.

- Clean a car before driving or pushing it into your workshop. Leave dirt outside.

- Consider a set of slave wheels and tyres to use when the car is not due to perform. This will save wear and tear on more expensive items, while narrow slave wheels and tyres may even help to get the car into a transporter.

- If you start a difficult job, vow to finish it before moving on to something easier, otherwise essentials may be forgotten.

- Keep things simple—that way you are likely to 'add lightness', but *don't* drill lightening holes willy nilly. If you don't know what you are doing you may save a few grams . . . you may also have a breakage. And talking of weight, know where the nearest weighbridge is. If you start becoming competitive you must have a car close to the minimum allowed weight—and you must have accurate

Tyrrell Racing Organisation – Car Setup Specification

Meeting	1990 Monaco GP		Session	WarmUp	
Circuit	Monaco		Length	3.328	km
Chassis Number	019/3		Driver	J.Alesi	
Date Issued	26-May-90		Date of Event		27-May-90

Engine

Type	Hart Special			Number	89103	
Exhaust System	Hart 4-1			Mixture	Set at circuit	
ECU No.		Limiter		11500	Map	DRB0025
Sparkbox No.		Limiter				

Gearbox		1st	1G	4K	Diff Rpm
Number	G019/1	2nd	14	32	2400
CWP Ratio	8,35	3rd	16	31	1750
Differential Type	Multiplate	4th	18	28	2260
		5th	19	24	2160
		6th	19	22	950

Chassis	Front	Rear	
Steering Rack	8 Tooth		
Rocker Springs	25/25, No Preload		
Push Rod Length	720	422	mm
Castor - set to...	2	4	deg.
Standard Ride Ht.	35	60	mm
'Horns' Std. Ride Ht.	25	36	mm
Camber @ Std. R/Ht.	2	0.5	deg.
Actual Ride Height	34	58	mm
'Horns' Ride Height	26	38	mm
Toes	0.5 In	0	deg.
Anti Roll Bar		None	

Brakes	Front	Rear
Brake Caliper	3557	3545
Brake Disc	1" Hitco	1" Hitco
Brake Pad	Hitco 442	Hitco 442
Master Cyl. Diameter	0.75"	0.75"
Brake Balance Set.	JA Std.	
Brake Duct Opening	Hole 6	Large
Brake Duct Blanking	None	None

Springs/Dampers	Front	Rear	
Spring Rate 1b/	3000	1550	
Damper Type	3012-1047	3012-1604	
Valving	BA73	BA53	
Set. Bump/Reb	2B2R	4B4R	
Bump Rubber Type	Koni 15mm	Koni 15mm	
Damper Free Travel	2	30	mm

Aerodynamics	Front	Rear	
Wing Type	GA1	Z38	
Setting	Hole 21	019 Mk2 Undertray	
Strip Flap	SF5/250		
Adjuster Setting	5 Reds		
Radiator Exit Ducts	Closed		
Water Radiator Type	Secan	Radiator Cap	13 PSI

Miscellaneous		
Driver Liquids	No	
Start Fuel	110	kg

If you learn by your experience you must know what spec a car was in on which event. The Tyrrell covered by this sheet took Jean Alesi to second place in Monaco in 1990. See the illustration on p.71 for the power curve of the engine used.

figures because you will be excluded if you are under weight.

- If you use a rolling road, try to keep using the same one—horses come in different sizes, as do the horsepower readings between rolling roads and you don't want to introduce variables.

Before you start preparing your car: check the regulations. Having done that, read them again. You will have to live with the rules and regulations for your particular racing class, and you must always be looking for ways round them. Don't think it is unsporting to do this—the interpretation of regulations is the whole essence of International motorsport. If you are not up to the latest tricks and tweaks, rest assured that someone else will be, and he will be the one taking the chequered flag.

Every set of regulations will imply that competitors will be deemed to have read and understood them, so ignorance is no excuse. If you get thrown out because you have been caught cheating (and it will be branded as cheating even if it is a misunderstanding) you will lose any championship points for the particular race, and may also lose any points you have scored up to then, even if you are not barred from the championship completely. If the offence is serious enough you can be fined and lose your licence for a period.

Support vehicles

Obviously, the type of vehicle you have to move your competition car around will depend on your budget; remember that the better your preparation the less support your car may need on events. You don't *have* to have two giant pantechnicons, one for the competition car and one to entertain sponsors in; races and rallies have been won by people taking their cars to events on trailers. The use of a trailer or transporter for a rally car is not a contradiction in terms, by the way, just commonsense because it saves wear and tear and, of course, enables you to get home after the event even if you breakdown or crash.

Whatever support vehicle you have, the spares and equipment you take must be properly stowed—stowed logically so that things are readily found, and stowed safely so that nothing can fly around and cause an accident in an emergency.

Don't overload a support vehicle with parts that are either unnecessary or don't actually fit your car. Sounds crazy? Yes, but many motorsport people are magpies and carry a load of junk around that would be useless on an event. Anything you carry must be 'ready to fit'—this could save time and win you an event

Loose parts flying around a support vehicle can be dangerous so stow things carefully, with heavy items low down. If you have more than one such vehicle, make the layout the same in them all.

later. Rolls of tape will of course be essential. Incidentally, be wary of buying second-hand parts, particularly moving ones. Because of the high cost of motorsport, and perhaps because of its air of danger and glamour, a percentage of parts seem to fall off the back of lorries. Be wary that you don't get caught in one of these rings; the police are fully aware of the costs of motorsport and won't be readily fooled.

If you are on a tight budget, it may be worth having a vehicle that has some form of sleeping accommodation, or maybe you could take a tent. Too uncomfortable for you? Perhaps that means you are not dedicated enough. One young Swede went into a hotel in Holland, realized that the cost of a room would buy a new tyre, slept in the car and bought the tyre. So what? you say. So with that attitude he went on to win the championship despite chronic lack of funds.

Is the support vehicle secure? Is it safe and roadworthy? And is it properly painted so that it is a credit to you and (we hope) any sponsors? Stress to any support crew that, having got a vehicle looking neat, they should not then clutter it with 'I've been over the Gross Glockner' stickers. A service vehicle should, however, carry a supply of stickers inside it, ready to give to kids or even help ease the way through customs.

Testing

Before moving on to consider the separate preparation needs of race and rally cars, let's spend a moment to consider some general points about *testing* that are common to both activities.

The first thing is to be clear on the team *management*. You can't control a backup crew while you are at the wheel, so someone else needs to be the Grand Fromage. Ideally, he should be a good administrator and organizer, firm enough to stop pits being cluttered with non-essential people, and with an eye for detail—like roping off a pit area or appreciating that a jack has to work when a tyre on a rally car is flat. He must know how many people can work on a car, where, and when. And he must ensure everyone else in the team knows.

Similarly, he must encourage clear lines of communication within a team on other matters—who is booking test facilities, fixing hotels, arranging passes, and so on. And, *above all*, who is allowed to authorize modifications to the car. Mods must be routed through one person to avoid chaos.

Having sorted out the command structure, there are other things for a driver to consider about testing:

- Take it seriously. Official practice or the first few miles of a rally are *not* the places to sort out a car.
- If you've been working all night to finish your car, try to find at least a few moments to *think* before you set off to test. Have you completed all the work? Did you tighten that critical nut and bolt? And so on.
- Keep records. Log settings, tyre pressures and temperatures, oil pressures, fuel used, and so on.

- Pay attention to safety. *Always* wear a helmet and seat belts. Always have someone else with you, preferably with first aid backup. If you are testing a rally car, then *all* the roads onto the section you are using must be blocked off; don't take as gospel a local's assurance that 'no one ever comes along that road'.

- Try to get someone who knows your type of car to drive it to give you an assessment.

- Ask experienced people to observe you on a track or stage: they may be able to pinpoint handling peculiarities or, more soberingly, oddball driving techniques. And having asked them to observe, listen to what they have to say.

- Start testing relatively slowly. Get everything, including you as the driver, warmed up before going quickly. Do four or five laps of a track or a few miles of a stage, then pause for a general spanner check and an inspection for water, oil, or petrol leaks.

- Next get a benchmark. The driver should be bright enough to do a run at a known 'rate of trying', i.e. at eight-tenths or whatever grade you use, and then you should change things *one at a time*. Obviously, if you need a suspension change and the gear lever knob keeps coming loose, then both of those could be attended to at the same time; but if you change, say, more than one setting at a time then you can go up blind alleys. Consider how often even the experts in Formula 1 admit they've lost their way in sorting a car ... then consider how much easier it will be for you to do the same. So: one thing at a time. At times you may even need to put the car back to its original settings as a cross check.

- You will need accurate timing equipment while testing but it doesn't *have* to be the latest ultra high technology piece of kit: a second is a second no matter how it is recorded. If you do have the latest timing equipment, do be sure you know how to use it.

- The driver, having set a benchmark, should try to be consistent when testing. If he is erratic, then times as well as modifications may be meaningless. As a driver you should be sufficiently self-aware to know if you are on form or not and whether, for example, the over- or understeer is due to you or the car.

- When testing, don't grind on forever. If you are clearly not making any progress, stop wearing the car out and pause for a think and maybe a phone round for advice.

- While you are out testing, under what approximate to on-event conditions, find time to practise wheel changing and, for the rally brigade, changing struts and so on. Establish who does what and, if possible, video a change so that you can study the operation later to seek improvements. Encourage mechanics to colour code their tools and to get into the habit of laying them (and other equipment) out in the same planned order each time.

- Finally, be honest with yourself and your support team. If you are slow because of an error on a corner, then admit it otherwise the times will confuse. And if, unhappily, you damage the car do at least have the grace to apologize to any support people who worked on it.

6

Preparing and Setting Up a Racing Car

If you are mechanically minded you may find the challenge of preparing a 'one-off' car invigorating, but life will be a whole lot easier if you have something more conventional from a reputable manufacturer. You should then be able to obtain a list of recommended settings for camber, castor, toe-in, ride height, and so on. If you buy a second-hand car that comes from one of the recognized manufacturers, visit them and get to know them. If you start to do well with the car they may even do a deal with you for reduced-price spares. Note the phrase 'if you start to do well'; that means *results.*

Without becoming a pain in the neck, try to get to know the works teams because they may make tiny changes from one race to the next and you must try to keep not more than one step away from them: two or three steps and you may be floundering at the back of the field. Find out where they are testing, what they experiment with, and find out if it is any good. In a refined art form like motor racing a small thing, which might cost only a couple of pounds, can make a difference. You must stay up to date and if you stay in close touch with the works team they may help you to incorporate the latest tweaks in your car, and perhaps help to give you a push if you are in the running for a championship. With some factories, you may be able to feed back information to *them*, because if you are seriously campaigning in one class of racing while they are concentrating on another, your intense effort in your particular formula may be greater than theirs.

Before preparing your car, go to races and study cars of the same type. Lie under them in the paddock if possible, make notes and take photographs. Talk to the drivers and team members if they seem approachable. If you look and learn, you should be able to incorporate all the best ideas into the preparation of your own car.

If you go to a circuit and watch the car you think handles best, then the one seems quickest on the straight, clearly you want the suspension of the handling car with an engine by the same tuner as the fastest car to give you the best chance to shine.

After absorbing all you can, when you start preparing a car for racing, whether it be a humble saloon or an F1 car, one basic principle applies and that is *attention to detail*. Think how often events are lost because of some trivial fault, most frequent of all being that elusive 'electrical problem'.

Anyway, vowing not to rush or skimp, and swearing allegiance to attention to detail, start your race car preparation by thinking of safety items.

Roll-over bars are crucial for most categories of racing, and with saloons and grand touring cars the extension down the windscreen pillars is almost as important as the one over your head, particularly if you somersault end over end. The best roll-over cage is likely to be the biggest roll-over cage, and remember that you can use the safety cage to stiffen the whole shell of a car if it is attached rigidly. Protection against lateral impact is essential and all in all this is one area where you should regard safety as more important than weight saving.

The main horror, apart from crashing, is of course fire, so have the best fireproofing you possibly can. Tanks should be isolated from the passenger compartment, ideally filled with foam, and if possible with a non-return valve so that if you have an accident the fuel supply automatically cuts off. Even if the regulations don't insist on a specific type of tank you should still get the best available. Although you should concentrate on the safety aspects, you should also look to the efficiency of a tank; you are not likely to win a race because of a brilliant fuel system, but you could very easily lose one because of a poor system.

Long-distance racing obviously presents its own fuel problems, where pit stops can win or lose a race, but in any sort of racing you will need to guard against fuel starvation when the fuel is thrown away from the pick-up point. You must also guard against dirt, which can clog up an engine; this means using filters when you are pouring petrol from churns. (Remember by the way that *all* filters on a car need changing on a regular basis.) You must be able to get all the fuel out of a tank because there is no point in carrying excess weight around with you. Clever systems are available for long-distance racing involving valves, so that a tank can be filled totally without any spillage. There is an added advantage in that if a driver sets off before the refuelling is completed, the pipe will simply pull out and the flaps close without any risk. If you have non-metallic fuel lines or vents passing through the driver's

If pit stops and rally service points are to run smoothly, they must be practised. Video practice runs for analysis later.

compartment they must be encased in a solid metal cover.

Don't treat safety regulations as something to which you have to pay lip service just to get through scrutineering; proper attention to safety can quite simply save your life. It can also make the difference between a car that is shunted yet barely damaged, and one that is a total loss. The only way you can lose every penny you have invested in a car is in a fire, because you can come away without a single salvageable item. Remember, fire extinguishers are not just for show.

If you fit a full fire protection system, it is worth making sure that when it goes off the pipes don't blow off, and that they distribute the fluid or gas to where it is supposed to go. Admittedly, it is rather expensive to set it off just to see that it is working, because you will have to buy a replacement charge, but at least make doubly sure that all the connections will take the pressure fed from the bottle. By the way, don't neglect to have a proper life support system linked to your helmet.

Continue your safety protection via good seat belts. When mounting them don't just put the brackets in the most convenient place: choose the strongest place. And if you are unlucky enough to have a major accident don't re-fit the seats or the seat belts without having them carefully checked by the manufacturers.

Having guarded your head with a roll-over bar, protected yourself against fire, and strapped yourself in, don't then try to save money or cut corners on brakes. For this reason be very careful that any re-runs of brake lines and pipes can't be chafed by seats or anything else on the car, and remember that a twin braking system is a lot safer than a single circuit. You will almost certainly modify the suspension, which may mean that you will have increased the travel in one direction or the other, so put the car on stands, take the springs off, and check that the brake pipes will stretch on full lock both ways to full stretch and to full bump. Similarly with the axle—jack the axle right up and right down, then jack it up fully on one side with the other side right down. In short, make sure that the brake pipes will reach in every possible angle and tangle into which the suspension can twist itself.

Remember that there is no restriction on the type of brake fluid used, so adopt the best competition type you can find.

Next, make sure that the things connecting you to the road, namely the wheels and tyres, are also safe. Ideally, the wheels should have safety humps in them, even if you can't fit safety studs. You may have to compromise over wheel off-sets, but try to get wheels that are as near as possible right without having to fit ridiculous spacers. If you are going to fit built-up wheels, especially second-hand ones, make sure that they haven't been bent and re-straightened. Watch for ageing on wheels, and above all, as in so many other things, try to use the same type as the leading drivers. Don't cut corners—at least not until you are actually on the track.

When you are fitting tyres it is worth checking the batch number. The competition fitters of the tyre companies work so hard that there is always a remote possibility that they might fit a couple of wrong tyres, and if you go out with a different mix on one side from the other you may think it is time you retired from racing.

Appreciate that suspension pick-up points and so on have to be strong because of the loading you will push through them with wide wheels and large slick tyres. This applies particularly to saloon cars, where the load is greater than the car was originally intended to take. Happily, there is an increasing move towards specifying maximum tyre widths to stop some of the lunatic developments in this area, which should also help to lower costs.

If you have bought a second-hand car you may find it worth replacing the ball joints. Don't just unscrew them at random, then go away to get new ones. Find out exactly what type you need (you will probably find the name and number etched on the joint) then take very close measurements of how it is installed on the end of the rod or wishbone, and make sure that you install the new one in exactly the same position. At least you will then end up with the car set something near right. Don't madly unscrew things without taking measurements.

For racing cars, you are unlikely to have a huge rev range on your engine so you need a selection of axle ratios to compensate for the different speeds of the circuits and the different tyre sizes. Again, don't go mad; a ratio that is nearly right will do for you until your driving improves. Get hold of someone who races one of your cars and try to find out which ratios he uses where, but do then take into account his tyre size.

As far as gearboxes are concerned, ideally you want something which, although possibly expensive, will be utterly reliable, so when drawing up your budget at the start of the season allow enough for a gearbox that is going to stand the pace; it will be cheaper in the long run.

But far beyond all the thought you put into preparation, a key factor in your racing career will be how well you tackle the magical process of 'sorting' or 'setting up' your car. In fact there is little magic in it, just hard work and application. Let's, by way of illustration, consider setting up a Formula Ford.

To begin with you have to know key facts about the chassis: you must know the ride height front and rear, the toe-in of the front and rear wheels, and their camber. And it's useful to know the wheelbase.

The first job is to make sure that the chassis is square. Disconnect the anti-roll bars and put the car up on trestles on a flat piece of ground. Use a spirit level to make sure it's level. From the centre of the lower suspension points drop a plumb-line to the ground. Mark the point where the line touches the ground exactly, and when you've done all the points, join them all together with a chalk line: then join all the diagonals and finally take a line through the centre. This line must pass through the centre of all the diagonals. Most modern racing chassis are built to a tolerance of $1/16$ inch or so; if yours proves to be out by more than this, it should be re-jigged by competent people. Incidentally, you should refer to the original manufacturer for basic dimensions—Ralph Firman at Van Diemen regularly gets such calls from people with cars built in the '70s! Perhaps another moral is to use cars for which the manufactuers (like Van Diemen) keep proper records.

Next, you can take the front and rear botom wishbones and make sure that the left-hand and right-hand units are identical. Then replace them, leaving off the spring and damper units. Put the chassis on the ground, again using the spirit level to make sure it's level, and use wooden blocks to raise it to the correct ride height front and rear.

Replace the wheels, and set to work in the following order of operations. Set the front castor (but not the rear castor at this point), check the tyre pressures and equality of tread depth, and make sure the wheels are not buckled. Disconnect the steering arms, and set the front camber with the wheels facing straight ahead.

When that is done, set the rear camber. Connect up the steering and set it at parallel, making certain that the distances from the ball-joint end of the track rod to the ball at the wheel end are absolutely equal on both sides. Then set the toe-in, using the gauge.

The rear toe-in is next: be warned that this is the most difficult and also the most important operation of the lot. There are four different types of adjustment, depending on the suspension design.

If the rear wishbone has its adjustment on the outside, the two lower radius arms must be taken off and made equal in length on both sides. All future adjustment can then be made from the wishbone adjustment point. Toe-in adjustment is made by lateral spacing of the inside joint: both radius arms must be equal in length.

If the suspension is of the twin parallel arm type, the forward arms on both sides will have to be taken off and made equal in length: all remaining adjustment is then done on the rear arms. If the lower wishbone has no provision for adjusting the toe-in, all the toe-in adjustment must be made on the lower radius arm.

The exact process is this: set up the car, and run a piece of string right round the car at hub height. Measure the width between the top outside edge of the two front tyres; repeat the operation for the two rear tyres, and then get a piece of wood of a thickness that is exactly half the difference between the track front and rear.

Adjust the rear toe-in on each side with the piece of wood stuck down between the string and the front hub, adjusting the rear wheels until the leading edge of the wheel just fails to touch the string. This has to be done equally on both sides, of course. Now check to find out what the setting is: use the toe-in gauge for this.

Set the wheels to parallel, achieving this by means of equal adjustments on both sides. Pack out or, if necessary, reduce the wooden distance piece until the string is once again just failing to touch the leading edge of the rear wheel. Then adjust both sides equally to the maker's recommendation: when it is right, the gap between the string and the leading edges of the wheels should be equal on both sides of the car. Make a note of the width of the piece of wood, and of the distance between the string and the leading edge of the wheel, and keep it in the toolbox.

Now you'll have to re-set the rear wheel camber by adjusting the top link, and you can set the castor of the rear wheels by adjusting the top radius arm. If no rear wheel castor setting is available from the manufacturer, put the spirit level across the bottom wishbone and adjust the castor until it is level. Then re-set the camber.

Back to the front of the car now to set the toe-in, making sure that the adjustment is equal on both sides.

The car is now basically set up, but we haven't quite finished: the next thing to do is to check the bump steer front and rear. For this we need the blocks of wood we used to fix the ride height, plus two more, so that we have two blocks around 6½ in thick and two only about ½ in thick. Drop the car on to the ½ in blocks front and rear, and check the toe-in. Then lift it right up on to the 6½ in blocks and check the toe-in once more. If the track is 'in' on the low position and 'out' on the high position, you need to drop the rack or raise the steering arm: if it is 'out' on the low blocks and 'in' on the high ones, then raise the rack or lower the steering arm. Carry out the same check in the same way at the rear of the car, aiming for zero difference between 'in' and 'out'.

If all the inner ball joints at the front are in line, it should follow that the outer ball joints are in line also, although the two 'lines' will be at different angles. And always keep the track-rods equal on both sides.

There are just a few points left now. Check the shock absorbers first: take the springs off the dampers, put a rod through the bottom joint, and by standing on the rod test the pressures down and up (bump and rebound) to make sure that they are equal front and rear. If the shock absorbers are provided with an adjustment, check it and make sure it works.

Check the lengths of the front and rear springs, then put them back on the dampers and replace the complete units on the car. If there was a difference in length, make a note of the difference and mark the spring. Set up the car to ride height with the driver aboard, bodywork on the chassis, and the fuel tank half full. If the springs were not equal side by side, find the difference by measuring one side and then the other and allow for the difference on the length of the springs. Check camber and toe-in after adjustments for bump steer.

Check that the car is level once again, then connect the anti-roll bar on one side. Adjust the other link until the roll bar bolts slip through, with equal adjustment on both sides. Do this back and front, with no tension on the roll bar.

Finally, the brakes. Check them first for balance: do this by disconnecting the bleeders on the front brakes and make sure there is full compensation on the balance bar when the pedal is pressed. The yokes must be far enough apart for the pedal to go right down. To adjust the braking—to get more braking effort on the front than on the rear, or vice versa—you must screw the rod of the balance bar (which passes through the upright part of the pedal, near the top) in the direction of the master cylinder for the braking circuit on which you need the increase. Do this in very small adjustments—it is very sensitive, and one turn at a time is sufficient.

And there you are—set up and sorted. All you have to do now is drive the thing. Different types of car may need different procedures but the meticulous attention to detail is essential whatever the vehicle.

The finer tuning of a car is part of the challenge of motorsport, but don't fiddle and experiment to the point of becoming neurotic. Sooner or later you have to get in and drive it. Before you venture off into too many exotic suspension tuning ideas it is worth finishing a race or two so that you have a benchmark of how the car performs against the opposition.

If you are sufficiently bright at sorting a car you will be able to get the springs made to your own liking. It helps when sorting a car if things are adjustable; if shock absorbers and roll bars can be adjusted it means that you can experiment much more easily without wasting a whole test session. If you can't get the car feeling right, and are able to persuade an experienced driver to try it, then at least he will be able to give you an idea of which direction to head if you have adjustable dampers. If nothing is adjustable it is difficult, even for an expert driver, to sample the car in one condition and pass a solemn judgement on what should be done before he has had the opportunity to change anything himself and draw a comparison.

When setting the car up, take into account how long you will be at the wheel. It may pay to settle for a set-up which, while slower over a short event, is better for a long-distance race because it is easier to handle.

Finally, after a test session water-protect the car, then clean it before you take it to scrutineering, putting your numbers and any sponsors' stickers on neatly. However busy you are, your car should always be well turned out. Last-minute panics are not the way to go motor racing.

And while we're on cleanliness, at the end of a hard race, where there's a lot of oil and rubber, clean the car the minute it comes in. If you leave oil deposits on the paintwork, and then try to clean it when you get back to the workshop, you will find that they have stained any light colours on the car. So don't forget, a quick wash over with petrol just to get the oil off before you leave for home.

Make a work list for the car between practice and a race, or between a heat and a final; it need not be an elaborate check list, just a simple bolt-tightening work list (in order of priority). When the car comes in the list should be worked through methodically

Be clean, be precise, be methodical in the way you lay out your car and equipment.

because in the heat of the moment little things can be forgotten. You will learn by experience which things loosen off, which things need adjusting, and which are liable to wear out; and as you learn, put them on the work list. Pilots use an extensive check list, so a simple list makes sense for motor racing, with one proviso: a blind grind through a work list must not stop a mechanic *thinking*, so that he can still spot trouble that may be cropping up for the first time.

If you move up the single-seater ladder you will need to learn how to work with wings on a car. Some circuits need them a lot, others hardly at all; but it is important to learn how to use them (or not use them, as the case may be) to the maximum advantage. Carefully measure the angles you use and find the best; then log them so that you are properly prepared the next time you visit that circuit. Wander through the paddock and look at the star drivers' cars and quietly put a degree gauge on to them to see what angles they are running, making sure that you only measure a car when it is on a level surface. Keep in mind the strength of the opposition before settling on how much wing to have on—you may need to be fast on the straights, at the expense of cornering, if they are the only places where you can overtake.

Engines

Engines have been left to last because, although power is obviously vital in winning races, you should never tune a car

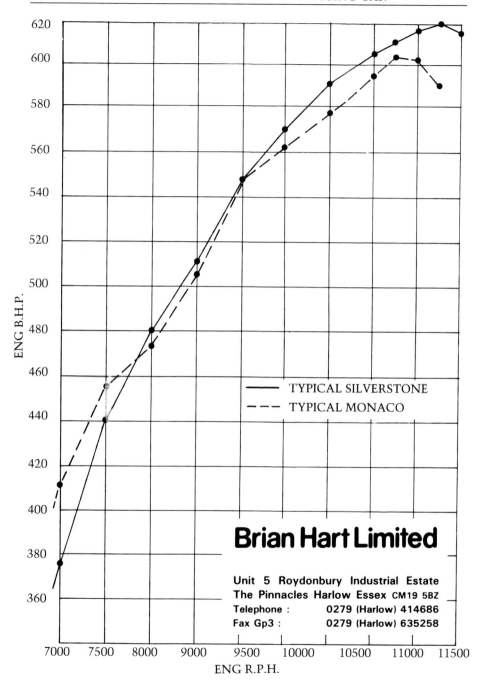

Power curves for two DFR F1 engines prepared for the 1990 season by the highly-respected Brian Hart. Note how the one for the twisty streets of Monaco performs better lower down at the expense of the top end. Mind, as Hart points out, Alesi tended to use the more powerful Silverstone spec most of the time!

further than your own ability is capable of handling. Don't let yourself be led into spending a fortune on engines until you have got the car handling and stopping properly, with a correctly sorted chassis and, above all, with your driving starting to show promise.

Before tuning an engine remember that it is not how much power you have but *where* you have it that is important, particularly on twisty circuits where torque is more important that absolute top-end power. Two minor things that cost nothing but can contribute to performance: ensure that you are getting full throttle and that your rev counter is accurate.

The key to engine turning for some saloon and single-seater races is 'blueprinting'. This term stems from the fact that engineering drawings were always prepared on blue paper, and blueprinting is simply a way of rectifying or modifying the parts to meet the dimensions foreseen by the designer. With the mass production of modern engines it is inevitable that the performance of basically identical units can vary quite a lot, so the key is to dismantle the engine, then put it together to the original drawings with loving attention to detail, all aimed at keeping friction losses to a minimum. The important thing is to have no projections that can interrupt the flow, but this is one area where it is important to

The sort of power shown on this Mountune Group A RS500 race engine for Rob Gavett would have looked good on F1 not too many years ago. Contrast the curve with the rally engine built by the same tuner (see p. 85).

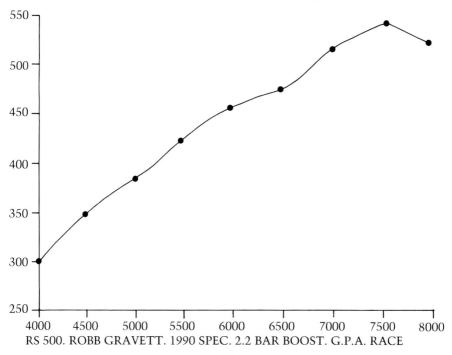

RS 500. ROBB GRAVETT. 1990 SPEC. 2.2 BAR BOOST. G.P.A. RACE

When you reach the dizzy heights of F1 you are unlikely to be working on your own engine. To be successful you will need a bank of technicians with a bank of computers.

be well aware of the scrutineer's attitude. Better to check first, before you start fettling away; fettling to tolerances on the homologation form might, if you come up against a bloody-minded scrutineer, make a car ineligible.

Pistons should be closely matched; weigh them carefully and, if there is any difference, grind metal away carefully from the heavier units until they are equal. Combustion chambers should obviously be well balanced: measure these with a burrette, then take a small amount of metal off the smallest chamber volume to bring it up to the largest. You may then have to machine a shaver off the head to bring the volumes back to standard, restoring the compression ratio at the same time.

When you move on to formulae with more elaborate engine tuning you will have to go to an expert, unless you have a great deal of knowledge as well as adequate facilities for doing your own work. The best advice is to look at who is winning, or at least finishing reliably and consistently, and then go to the tuners of those engines for your own power unit. Incidentally, if you can afford the luxury of a spare engine to take to races, it must be race prepared so that if necessary you can drop it in and go racing with it straight away.

Finally on engines, remember that the cheapest deal may not give you the best results, and don't necessarily go to the tuner who does the most vociferous promotion, either via PR or advertising. Few engines run purely on hot air.

7

Preparing and Setting Up a Rally Car

Before starting the preparation of a rally car, be quite clear what sort of events you are going to use it on. Are you going to do tarmac rallies, which hopefully will be relatively smooth, or are you intent on full-blooded stage events, where you'll be banging about on rugged roads? Another consideration, of course, is whether you'll have to use the car for business, or even for the wife's shopping, between rallies.

Next, study the regulations. Are you going to run in events for cars tuned under FIA Group N (supposedly standard) or Group A (more modified) rules, or are you pitching into a championship with its own unique regulations? On many club events, provided the car is safe, you will have virtually a free hand over preparation, although you must bear in mind that European legal regulations for cars—emissions, noise levels, and so on—are creeping in and will ultimately hem in rallyists very severely.

Having decided the type of events you are going to do and the group you intend to compete in, check the regulations before doing anything else; bear in mind that if you have a new car, any competition activity will almost certainly make the warranty null and void.

If you have the time and money, strip your car down to the bare shell. If you are buying a fresh car and intend to subject it to this treatment, then wheel and deal at garages, because a few hundred demonstrator miles, or a few paint scratches, are not likely to bother you, and you might get a price reduction accordingly. Buy a car without a sunroof by the way.

Having stripped the car, remove all the manufacturer's underseal and sound deadening material to save weight and then weld the shell to strengthen it—stitch weld the seams for 1 in every 2 in, ie 1 in welds with 2 in gaps between them. Sounds simple? Well, yes, but before doing so check with the manufacturers just what is allowed and, above all, recommended, and do keep in mind that if you weld without proper thought you may simply be adding weight to no effect.

Before starting on the shell, natter to some of the people who regularly rally your type of car; most of them will be only too eager to go on at some length about where and how the body breaks and needs attention. While you have the car stripped down, fit the fireproof bulkhead behind the back seat. This is also the time to do any suspension modifications that may involve welding and cutting and shutting.

The single most important item to fit is a full interior roll cage, and this is the one area where you shouldn't try to save either weight or money; it can make the difference between walking or being carried away from an accident. Be sure the cage you fit is one that will protect you properly if you have a shunt and is to an approved specification. Pad the roll bar where you are likely to bump against it (the rubber tubing used to insulate central heating pipes is ideal), and take particular care to cover any nuts and bolts that stick out.

Now pay attention to weather-proofing around the body seams and block all holes to keep out dust, water, and heat. Rally cars inevitably get grimy and grubby, but the more you can do to keep out the elements the better for both you and the car.

Having completed the shell preparation, you now come to one of the most underrated and over-bodged jobs of all—the electrics. *Plan* in advance and think about where everything is going to go and keep the following in mind:

- Avoid crisscrossing the car with the loom.
- Avoid unnecessary connections; they add weight and can go wrong. Make the ones you do use grease-free and tight fitting.
- Always use the correct specification of wire with different colours to aid identification.
- Use grommets in all holes to prevent wires chafing.
- Clip wires in place, don't leave them hanging around.
- House fuses in easily reached positions, ideally away from intense heat.
- Always use the correct amperage fuses. Don't be tempted to use an oversize fuse to overcome an overload problem; this is defeating the whole point of having a fuse in the first place.

Electrical faults are the most common and most irritating causes of failure. Protect against problems by using the correct grade of colour-coded wire, properly fitted and mounted.

With the electrics handled, now fit a guard to protect the sump of the engine. It should be properly fitted and mounted to the side rails. If you are using an expensive magnesium or Kevlar sumpguard, you can prolong its active life by putting a plate of mild steel underneath to take the brunt of the abrasive effect of stones. Attach the steel plate with self-tapping screws, which must be fitted in such a way that they're not protruding and therefore cannot get ground away. It's cheaper to replace a steel sheet every so often than have to renew a complete and expensive guard.

If you are the boffin type, then you may want to get involved in your own suspension experiments, but you'd be better advised watching what the works or leading private entrants do, following them as closely as you can.

Replace all suspension bushes with heavy-duty ones designed for competition use. If the regulations permit, and there's one available, fit a high-ratio steering rack to help when you are doing your arms-crossed, mind-bending routine, although it shouldn't come too high up your list of priorities if funds are limited.

Apart from driver stupidity, more cars probably drop out of rallies through back axle trouble than anything else. Give yourself a better-than-average chance by making sure that your axle is properly assembled and properly located.

If you can get heavy-duty springs and bushes for your car, then obviously you should fit them, but bear in mind that the spring weights and ride heights you need will depend on the type of rallies you are going to do. The tendency may be to run the car high to give increased protection, but this is likely to impair the handling.

If there is a choice of axle final-drive ratios you should try to find out what the leading contenders in your type of car are using. There are sometimes heated discussions before rallies between engineers who want high final-drive ratios in the hope of improving reliability and drivers who want low ratios, ie those which are numerically higher, so that they'll have better acceleration with a lower maximum speed. We don't want to totally kill your creative urge but once again . . . use what the leading cars do.

You need to consider gearbox ratios when deciding on final drives, and bear in mind that if you fit too high a ratio your theoretical maximum speed will never be reached, simply because the laden rally car will never give its engine the chance to pull to that speed.

Next, consider the drive shafts. On rough events these will be given shock loads in the order of three times normal, and you must try to ensure that you have the most up-to-date specification. Even this is no guarantee of reliability because it's an area in which all works teams hit trouble from time to time. Make sure the shafts have no sharp changes in section, polish out any deep scratches or radiused edges, and if possible crack-test them before each major event. Check the joints, keep a log of the life of your drive shafts, and if in any doubt try to change them frequently.

A limited-slip differential is a must if allowed by the regulations; make sure that it is correctly set and be sure to use the right oil. If you have the time and facilities, it's worth 'running in' an axle on a hack car driven gently for a few hundred miles.

If you don't have problems with drive shafts, the next area where you might hit trouble is the gearbox. As well as fitting the most appropriate gear ratios it is worth taking some trouble to make sure that the selectors are in reasonable condition so that you can make quick, easy changes. If you're going to modify the engine extensively (which may in some cases double the power) you will probably have to go up to whatever alternative gear ratios are listed for competition use by the car manufacturer. This in turn may mean that you'll need a special bell-housing, which will increase the cost, but you might find a lightweight magnesium version available, which will at least reduce the weight.

We appreciate that a lot of this chapter aims at the ultimate and therefore involves cost, but you'll appreciate that you don't *have* to have all these things; the important thing is to keep everything in perspective and if possible develop the car as your own driving ability improves. Above all, it is always better to settle for less power if it will help you to maintain reliability.

You may find yourself chasing troubles up and down the transmission, which brings us to the clutch. You can obtain competition clutches for most cars; if you fit a really vicious one, which is either in or out, it will be somewhat unsuitable for normal road use, particularly with the higher pedal pressure needed to overcome the increased spring load.

Make sure that the release bearing is man enough for the increased loading—a common cause of breakdown. To some extent the life of a clutch is in your hands (or feet) as the driver; many have been destroyed simply by the antics of people manoeuvring cars onto trailers.

Having sorted out the axle, gearbox, and clutch, the prop shaft should be properly balanced because if it isn't it can cause more aggravation than you've really got time for before a rally. A jubilee clip round the prop shaft, moved until the heavier part corrects the out-of-balance condition, can sometimes give you short-term relief. Check the universal joints and bearing carriers.

If you think this is all rather complicated for rallying, imagine yourself as the engineer for a team trying to win a Safari, where you need a bottom gear that will pull you out of mud at low speed, and a top gear that will allow you to cruise comfortably at well over 100 mph—all this in a temperature hot enough to melt normal bushes and give drivers brain fade.

A lot of people get very concerned about making their cars go well; they should pay more attention to making sure that they stop well. Brake pipes—which should be 'Aeroquip' type—should be well protected and routed inside the car where possible. If you do put them inside, make sure they can't be damaged or flattened by the seats or other heavy objects (such as your co-driver's big feet).

Washers and seals in the cylinders and calipers should be replaced regularly, particularly if an extra servo is built into the system. Brake discs should be running true and be in good condition, and it goes without saying that wheel bearings should be checked frequently and properly maintained. Brake problems are often caused by knock-off as a result of worn or maladjusted bearings. You'll gradually build up a simple check list of such things to check on the car before every major event.

Ideally, a rally car should have a dual-line braking system, ie one with twin master cylinders, either working in tandem (one operating through the other) or, better, a parallel system using two separate cylinders side-by-side with an adjustable swinging beam between the two; one cylinder operates the front brakes, the other the rear. The front-to-rear braking ratio can be adjusted by means of the balance bar (or by varying the master cylinder sizes) so that the brakes in effect can be 'tuned' to suit the driver. They can be changed during an event if, say, a driver wants to adjust his braking ratio to cope with a tarmac stage after being on loose surfaces. Aim to have the feel of the brakes right with the balance bar in its middle position so that you have the maximum flexibility should you want to adjust during a rally. However, until you are very good you won't need this degree of sophistication, so settle for a happy compromise in which you have confidence. A twin system obviously gives greater safety should either circuit fail. If you use a parallel dual-line braking system and you want to fit servos, you must fit a separate one for each circuit because a single servo would reduce the system to a single circuit.

Obviously, you'll want harder competition brake pads; most of the with-it brake companies have efficient competition departments who will be able to give you advice both on brake material and on brake fluid. Competition pads should always be bedded in before an event. (By the way, bed in new discs with old pads, or new pads with old discs—*not* new with new.) If, as is likely, you will be changing pads during an event, then bed the spares in too. Incidentally, most drivers prefer a fly-off handbrake; it's usually fairly simple to modify the action of the ratchet to achieve this.

If you can afford them, you'll probably want to go to magnesium wheels; if you stay with standard wheels have them crack-tested regularly, and renew them if necessary—cheaper than buying a new body shell because a broken wheel puts you off the road. Aluminium wheels may look prettier than standard wheels, but they can sometimes be heavier, which isn't the object of the exercise at all.

Don't go mad on wheel widths; a lot of the Scandinavian experts use quite narrow tyres, especially when there is a lot of snow, because if you are the odd-ball with wide tyres you'll find that no one has helped to make tracks through the snow into which your tyres will fit. There should always be spare wheel nuts on board the car and one, or preferably two, wheel braces in a clearly known and accessible place. The jack should also have a specific and convenient place in the car; bear in mind that it has to lift new and possibly studded tyres as well as raising a car on a flat tyre, so it must have plenty of travel. Keep in mind, too, that jacks wear out like everything else so check the efficiency of yours from time to time.

Unsprung weight is not referred to very much with rally cars, but it probably makes just as important a contribution to roadholding as in racing, which is another reason for thinking carefully before becoming involved in mad modifications to brakes, wheels, and so on.

Now you've got the body shell strengthened, painted, wired, and with much of the running gear in, it's time to turn to the interior. Seats are a matter of individual taste but they should be strong, securely bolted to the floor, obviously comfortable, and with good lateral support. There must be no play in the seat at all, so delete the fore and aft runners. If the co-driver finds your preferred driving position uncomfortable, tough. The seats should of course have head restraints for safety as well as for relaxation.

Both crew members should have good seat harnesses, properly fitted (see photographs) and mounted, ideally with straps passing through the seat and not round it.

The steering wheel is up to you, but now that there are strict European regulations on safety it makes sense to go for a safe rather than a pretty one. Thank God those lethal wood-rimmed ones which splintered in accidents have died out. Remove the anti-theft device on the steering column but do keep a careful guard on your car; too many have had bits pinched off them, especially (ghoulishly) when left after a crash.

When it comes to instruments there's really no need to blindly follow the works cars or to kit a car out like a space capsule; this can be unnecessarily expensive and time wasting. When did you last have a failure with any of the instruments in a standard car? Probably never, and there's no reason to suppose that they will automatically fail under the tougher conditions of a rally. Some of the works cars have large, very bright warning lights fitted for alternator and oil pressure, but then their large, not very bright drivers mask the lights.

If you have an oil pressure warning light, make sure it warns you before the damage is done, say at a minimum of 25 psi.

The co-driver will probably feel feel happier with a strong bracing bar for his feet so that he can rigidly push himself back into his seat. It's worth fitting a thin box in the space just in front of the navigator's seat (ie underneath his thighs) to take spare bulbs and sweeties. It can also provide stowage for the road book and route card—although these are probably better in a simple door pocket or under a clip or rubber band on the sun vizor. If the stowage box has a lock fitted it can be used for stowing passports, etc. The co-driver will also feel happier with matt black everywhere to reduce reflection, as well as with whatever distance/time measuring device has caught his eye. Developments

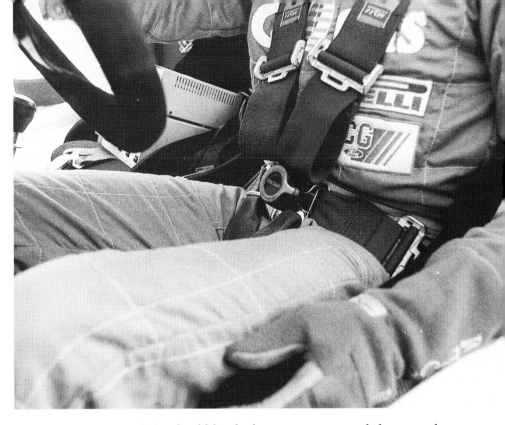

Above and below *Seat belts should be the best you can get and they must be properly mounted. Note how they have ridden up in the second photograph where they are* incorrectly *fitted.*

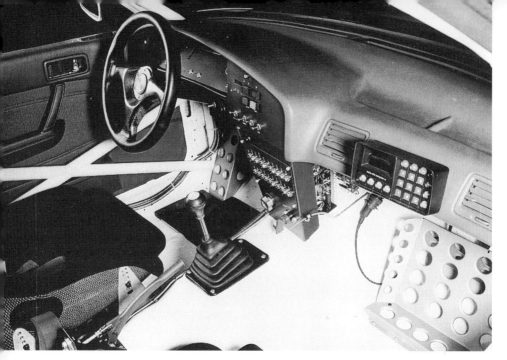

Note the timing equipment and co-driver's foot brace in this purposeful Prodrive-prepared Subaru.

in this area are likely to be as rapid as in the computer world as a whole; *but* remember you don't have to have something that's been developed for a space shuttle provided what you do have is legible enough and accurate enough for the co-driver to 'manage' the car.

You sometimes see pictures of single-seater drivers being fitted for their cars: it's worth taking the time to do this for rallying. The driver should get into the car, belt himself in, and check that he can reach all the appropriate switches, pedals, etc. In particular he must be able to reach the ignition switch when belted in. Group auxiliary switches in clusters of no more than three, so that you will be able to find a particular switch without too much groping and fumbling. To improve crew comfort, make sure that the heating and demisting systems work properly. Although night driving is now fairly rare on rallies (the poor dears have to get proper rest, you see) you should fit the best lights you can get and use under the regulations; have auxiliary lights quickly detachable so that they can be carried in service vehicles when not in use in order to save weight.

Whatever the regulations, follow as far as possible what the experts are using, and make sure that any auxiliary lamps are mounted in accordance with legal requirements. Use the right size wire for the job and build relays into the circuits to cope with the loading. When mounting auxiliary lamps be sure to use firm brackets—there's nothing more distracting than lights that wobble about on every bump. Don't run with Blackpool illuminations on the front without an adequate alternator.

With an improved alternator, make sure your fan belt is strong enough to drive it; preferably have twin pulleys with two fan belts. Fan belts should be run in for a few miles before an event to take the stretch out of them, and then they should be re-adjusted. Run in a spare belt and then keep it clipped somewhere convenient under the bonnet, ideally in such a way that it is already laced over any awkward pulleys.

Check the throttle cable; all too often you read of drivers having to finish stages with their co-drivers under the bonnet operating the throttle control, which is desperately undignified, particularly as they invariably have a split in the seat of their trousers.

Fit a stop under the accelerator pedal so that it is not possible to push it past the maximum travel of the throttle linkage, thus putting too much strain on the nipples. But caution: make sure it is not then possible for the throttle pedal itself to jam against this stop—it has been known to happen (all too often). You should change throttle springs regularly and always have at least two of them, with a spare mounted somewhere under the bonnet. Also, don't overstretch them. Remember that the cheapest way of tuning a car is to make sure that you can get full throttle.

While all this activity is going on around and under the bonnet, it is worth fitting bonnet catches so that the lid cannot fly up just when you've started a special stage.

When you move to the boot of the car, neatness should be the cry. If the battery is in there, make sure that it is firmly clamped down (the same applies even if it's beneath the bonnet), and the battery tray should be bolted to the body rather than relying on tack welding. A heavy spare wheel flailing around in the boot can do a lot of damage, so make sure it is securely fastened and mounted, yet easy to get out quickly. A tubular pillar welded to a 6-inch square of 16-gauge mild steel, which is then bolted to the floor of the boot, will locate the centre of the wheel, which can then be secured by elastic cords. Wire a key permanently into the boot lid lock so that you don't have to fumble about when you're trying to get into it in a hurry, which you will be when you have a puncture.

Fuel lines should be of the 'Aeroquip' type and while bag tanks are desirable, if expensive, remember that car manufacturers have to work to pretty stringent regulations in this field, so that normal fuel tanks are reasonably safe. Wing tanks can be more vulnerable than tanks in the centre of the boot if, as is likely, you're in the habit of bouncing off banks to help you get round corners.

If you are paying attention to weight, you will rarely be carrying spare petrol, but if ever you are cans should not be kept loose on the boot floor but should be properly stowed. Locking petrol caps can waste a lot of time on rallies—delete yours.

You will need an external switch for the electric circuit which must be marked clearly. You should, of course, have a fire extinguisher on board, and if you can afford it it's worth having an elaborate plumbed-in system that will put out boot and bonnet fires. Ensure your car has strong, clearly marked towing hooks; too many breakdown companies have done more damage to a rally car pulling it out of a ditch than the driver caused getting it in there in the first place. You may consider carrying a pair of simple goggles in case the screen pops out, as well as old gloves to help when changing pads or wheels; but care: *don't* clutter the car with everything but the kitchen sink. Only carry minimal essentials.

Have some simple stowage system—such as a net or padded box—for your crash hats so that they can't roll about. Leave the carpets out as well as the heavy sound deadening felt; apart from reducing the fire risk, such materials smell if they get wet and soggy, although with the aromas that arise in the average rally car you probably won't notice this.

If you've got this far without falling asleep or going bankrupt we can now turn to engine tuning. This has been deliberately left to the end of preparation because power isn't the be-all and end-all of rally success, and tuning should be approached from this point of view.

If you intend to tackle your own engine tuning—and it's not really recommended—remember that good mid-range torque is more important than anything else. An engine with good top-end performance but little else can be an embarrassment on loose stages, and could affect reliability if it meant that you were constantly having to use high revs. If you go to an outside engine tuner, go to one who has a reputation for reliability. You want someone who gives consistent value for money, rather than a fly-by-night boy wonder who happens to claim the most extravagant horsepower.

A basic improvement in engine performance for Group N can be obtained by stripping and rebuilding the power unit to precise tolerances as discussed under blueprinting in the previous chapter. How far you go in blueprinting must be between you, the regulations, and your conscience; this is one area where different interpretations of Group N between different countries can sometimes lead to problems with scrutineers and accusations of cheating.

If you move away from Group N and over to the freer Group A (where the outright winners invariably come from) then the prime

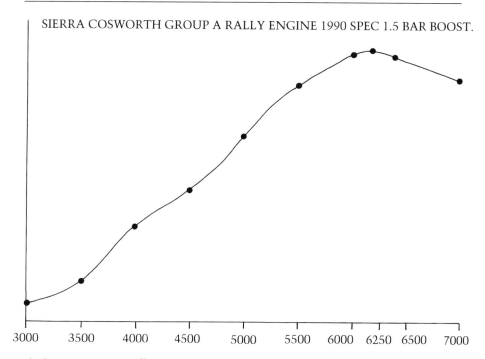

SIERRA COSWORTH GROUP A RALLY ENGINE 1990 SPEC 1.5 BAR BOOST.

3000   3500   4000   4500   5000   5500   6000 6250 6500   7000

A Group A Sierra rally engine prepared by Mountune. Compare this with the race engine illustrated on p. 72.

objective should be to improve gas flow, and the magic operation under these regulations is 'machining and polishing'. Although, through a restrictor, FISA hope to keep maximum power on rally cars to 300 hp you will still be increasing the power quite substantially and if you aren't totally sure of what you are doing, go to an expert otherwise the resultant 'bang' will be an expensive one.

One of the most important things you can do to improve the reliability of an engine doesn't affect the power at all; fit a dry-sump lubrication system *if* it is allowed (as it may only be under the freer club regulations). With a main oil reservoir, properly designed and baffled, fitted remote from the engine (safely in the boot, for instance), and with the existing sump replaced by a shallower type with an oil-collection function rather than an oil-storage one, the system will cut out the oil surge that can lead to bearing starvation and will allow for a higher oil capacity, which in turn will result in lower oil temperatures. A two-stage pump takes oil from the tank and pumps it directly into the main oil gallery. There is a case for dry sumping being allowed in any rally class because of the improved reliability and, hence, reduced costs.

Petrol quality is fairly uniform across Europe these days, but if you know you will be travelling through some of the more remote areas you should find out in advance what the octane rating will be, and repare your engine with this in mind. If rallying has any concern for its public image (and one sometimes wonders) then lead-free fuel needs to be made mandatory.

Moving away from the engine itself (having sprayed the electrics with a damp proofer), next turn to the exhaust system, which in a rally car is one of the most important parts of all—if only because, next to lights, noise causes more public irritation than anything else. If we are to keep the sport alive, then competitors may have to get used to turning up with cars that are *quieter*, if anything, than even standard versions. Anyway, to cut the sermonizing, check that the joints between the various sections of the exhaust system slide apart easily so that you can change damaged sections without having to fit a completely new system.

A chapter on car preparation could go on for ever. Make sure no self-tapping screws go through body panels where they can snag or chafe on pipes, wires, or tyres. A small point, which again sums up what rally preparation is all about: attention to detail.

When the car is complete, double-check that you've adequately water-protected it; if necessary, play a garden hose under the bonnet as a test.

Before you take it on an event, run the car in, then shake it down at rally speeds. If it won't stand a couple of brisk miles over a rough local track, it's not likely to survive a rally. It's amazing how often even the professionals spend the first few hours of a rally finishing and fettling their cars. Having shaken it down, check it over again; even works drivers have slipped up by forgetting to check that they've got the spare fan belt, jack, or wheelbrace on board. When this happens it's the crew's fault, because it is their job to double-check all essentials so that even if the mechanics have slipped up an error is spotted in time.

Finally, when you are happy with the car, clean it before you take it to scrutineering, and attach any sponsors' stickers neatly. Quite apart from the positive impact on sponsors, well turned out cars avoid the risk of a negative impact on the public, which is even more important.

However well you may have prepared your car, from time to time you will still run into trouble. When this happens, bear in mind that even if the works teams have their mechanics out on the rally route, they are likely to be concentrating entirely on their own cars. This may seem a bit tough at the time, but it is understandable when you pause to remember that works teams are in an event to win outright. This means that if you are a serious rallyist you will need to provide your own service vehicle although don't do this if service is banned by the regulations.

When planning a service vehicle keep the following in mind:

- Consider uprated springs and shock absorbers because of the extra weight the vehicle will be carrying.
- Keep the vehicle itself well serviced. Brakes in particular must be in top condition.
- Don't overload the service vehicle. Don't carry anything that takes so long to fit that the rally car will be out of the event anyway.
- Parts should be stowed safely in known positions so that they are readily to hand. Heavy parts should obviously be kept on or near the floor. Small items should be kept in drawers, clearly marked.
- Have lead lights plus general lighting mounted high on the service vehicle.
- Assume it will rain so carry protective clothing as well as something to lie on in mud.

Service crews should try to arrive at their service point early to get the best position, and they should choose places to avoid annoying the public; don't service outside someone's house unless the occupants have given you permission. If you are servicing near a control it's probably tactful not to use the officials' table as a workbench. In any event, mechanics need to be briefed about where they are *not* allowed to service.

On arrival at a service point, the crew should check the rally's direction of approach, which should have been given them by the co-driver, and they should then put out the items they will need— jack, oil, tools, etc.

There should always be at least two people, preferably both mechanics, at a service point, and the workload should be planned. What needs doing may have been fed through by radio otherwise one service person should go straight to the driver to see what special work needs doing while the other starts a routine service. The co-driver should put the service requirements into an order of priority, which is one of the advantages of having radio; if the co-driver can radio ahead that the car needs two cans of petrol and a spare tyre it can save precious seconds, and may save having to do the next section in the dust of a car which overtakes you while stopped for service.

Prioritization is important because it's no use spending time refitting a pedal rubber if the differential needs changing. Sometimes a major job, such as a gearbox change, will have to be planned over several service points: start clearing the decks at the

Above *Tools should be colour coded so that mechanics can find their own after a hectic stop. Note the power point on the side of the service vehicle.*

Below *Ideally, schedules should allow adequate time to set up a service point before rally cars arrive. Note the long power lead.*

first, swop the box at the second, tidy up the car at the third, and so on. It helps if mechanics have practised changing key items beforehand. Apart from sorting out 'who does what' the procedure may also throw up the need for a specially adapted tool to reach an awkward place and it will also give you an idea of how long certain jobs take. The more the known jobs are practised, the more time there will be to solve the awkward, unexpected problems.

Mechanics should never be idle at a service point because even if drivers don't need anything in particular they should always be carrying out preventive maintenance. Small things are important—mud or snow cleared from under wheel arches will avoid a dangerous build-up, for example. Check, check, then check again.

Service mechanics need to be able to improvise; they may have to do things that would normally make engineers wince, but they shouldn't go to the extent of taking risks with the safety of the crew. If they've got to do major work on a car it may help to push it on to its side, but take care to watch fluid levels. If they start any welding, have a fire extinguisher ready and have one, too, when refuelling, which is often the main, sometimes the only, reason for a particular service point.

Mechanics should check their service plan before an event and query any schedule that looks impossible. They must do this before a rally starts, because once under way it is imperative that they get to every place—a crew may have based their fuel plans on the assumption they will be getting some from their service crews. Service schedules should never be set at more than 25 mph average, because it takes time to pack a service car when the rally has gone through. As an aside—are the mechanics reasonable drivers? If not maybe they should go on a course.

Service mechanics should be clearly briefed on prohibited areas and any other specific rules and regulations that affect them. It is in the competing crew's interests to see that this is done because even inadvertent misdemeanours by mechanics could result in problems with organizers for the rally car itself.

Mechanics should keep service cars in reasonably shipshape condition, otherwise it becomes impossible to find things; above all they must take their rubbish with them. Leaving debris outside people's houses is a sure way of rousing hostility to rallying.

8

On Track

As recommended back in Chapter 2, before going racing it's worth taking a course at a school. Such courses are a lot less costly than buying your own car and then perhaps finding that racing is not for you. However, don't be misled into thinking that because, say, an F1 driver passed through a racing school at the start of his career a similar destiny automatically awaits you. It's not that easy, although a course will give you a basic grounding in racing driving technique, which will stop you being a complete innocent at large (possibly even a dangerous one) during your first events.

It's almost too obvious to warrant mention, yet it seems to escape a lot of drivers' attention: read the rules! Understand exactly what the regulations say and mean, particularly with reference to the correct passes, licences, record cards, etc, and above all keep up to date on flag signals; they are designed to make racing safer for everyone, including you.

If you misunderstand a particular signal not only could you cause yourself harm but, even worse, you could injure someone else. A medical will have shown whether or not you are colour blind, and therefore may have particular problems over flag signals. Needless to say, having understood the signals you should always obey them; the in-fighting that goes on for works drives has led to hooligan driving in some racing categories. Lack of knowledge of the law will be no excuse if you are a transgressor.

Signals from your own pit are hardly mandatory, but you must know exactly how to interpret them and you should agree with your pit crew in advance what information you need. Time gaps to the cars ahead and behind you will be more important than lap times, and laps to go more important than laps completed. Remember that if you are a slow runner you may complete less laps than the winner.

Get into the habit of performing a cockpit drill before an event, just like a pilot, and above all be comfortable in your race car because this can breed confidence. When you climb into a single-seater for the first time it may seem a long way to the front of the car, and you may become mesmerized by seeing the front wheels flapping about, but you'll soon get used to these things as well as the low driving position. Go to a lot of trouble to get the car set up exactly as you want it, with everything nicely to hand. You must be able to see all the gauges without having to move your head to see past the steering wheel, and you must cultivate the habit of reading the dials. Make sure that you can reach all the switches when you are strapped in; the ignition switch and fire extinguisher button must be particularly accessible.

Position the gear lever so that it is absolutely right for you, making sure that your knuckles don't rub on the body of the car when changing gear; check that you can get your hand round the gear lever knob in all its positions. Pad any protrusions that could cause you discomfort during a race.

Take a similar amount of trouble over the positioning of your pedals; for this you should always wear your race shoes, which may have an entirely different feel from your normal footwear. The pedals should be spaced exactly the correct distance apart, and if they are not adjustable they should be bent appropriately to make 'heeling and toeing' easier (actually this is something of a

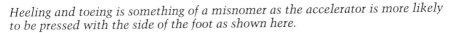

Heeling and toeing is something of a misnomer as the accelerator is more likely to be pressed with the side of the foot as shown here.

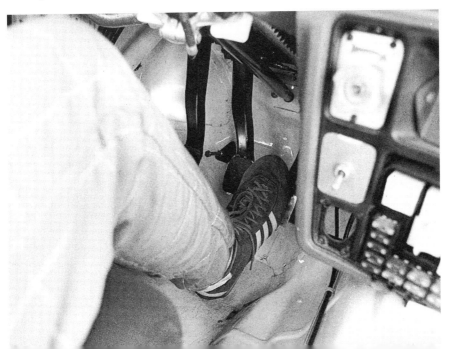

misnomer because in the confined space of most racing cars the 'toeing' will be done with the side of the foot).

Most of the 'feel' you have in a racing car comes from your buttocks and your heel and/or foot rest, so it is vital that such rests are in exactly the right places, positioned so that your feet automatically drop on them. Try to ensure that there is adequate space for your feet. If there isn't, you may get cramp, which will take the edge off your concentration and hence your driving, and could even become dangerous. Incidentally, whilst on the subject of pedals, if you feel that the clutch is not clearing properly, before stripping it down make sure that the engine mixture is absolutely right and that the engine is revving correctly with the throttle. If it hesitates, albeit only fractionally, you'll find that the gears may crunch, but the fault may not be with the clutch but with the engine.

If you have to double-declutch, the only way to learn how to do this successfully is to start slowly then gradually work up speed until it becomes an automatic reaction between your arms and legs—in other words co-ordination, which is really what a lot of driving is all about. Similarly, you'll learn how much to rev the engine when changing down. In racing cars with the normal dog-type rings you must be able to get a clean clutch change, otherwise you'll wear the rings out, which can become expensive.

If you've been brought up as a motor racing enthusiast you'll probably have starry ideals of legendary drivers of old doing the long, straight arm bit at the wheel. You may be able to do this in a little sports car with narrow wheels, but in modern racing cars where the steering is heavier you will probably have to sit closer to the wheel. Wherever you sit, you need plenty of support from your seat. The support should be as high up your back as possible, otherwise if you have just your backside in the seat your spine will be supporting all the load of the steering before it is transmitted to your nerve centre, namely the aforementioned buttocks. So find a seat that hugs you right up underneath your arms, and even up to your shoulders if this is possible, because it will take a great deal of tiring effort out of driving. If your stomach muscles are working all the time while you are racing it can make you really tired.

Make sure you have the best seat belts and that they are adjusted to suit you because they will help to hold you in the seat; the tighter they are the safer they are. If you start a race with the belts loose they will become progressively looser as you bounce up and down; in a long-distance race, when you are sweating a lot, you may even become marginally thinner, which will affect the tightness of the belts. Of course, in long races with two drivers per car, the adjustment and fitting of belts can become more

Above and below *The principles of seating are the same for race and rally cars: you must be able to reach the top of the steering wheel without stretching; you must be able fully to depress the pedals with your back against the seat; you must be able to operate the gear lever without having to lean forward. Whether you sit well back (as above) in what looks like a nice comfortable position, or closer (as below) is up to you. For what it's worth, the lower position seems increasingly in vogue with rally drivers from Southern Europe.*

complicated; in this case, if the two drivers are very different in stature, you may have to accept some form of compromise.

Before you take your newly acquired toy into a race, make sure that you get in some private practice to shake down both the car and yourself. You can do this on public test days, although if you can afford it a private test session will enable you to do a more comprehensive job. But, to repeat earlier advice (because it is so important), if you hire a circuit privately, never ever test on your own, and never ever without someone knowing where the doctor, ambulance, hospital, and telephone are located. Sadly, people get killed testing; the safety precautions need to be as elaborate on these occasions as during a race meeting.

If you are going to a circuit you know to be bumpy you may need to raise the ride height to stop the car bottoming, but don't forget that this can affect the handling unless it is done correctly. Keep a log of your suspension settings as well as tyre wear, temperatures, and so on; above all, keep a record of gear ratios because these will play a key part in your success. Like so many other things in racing they may have to be a compromise.

If you are starting absolutely from scratch, talk to the manufacturers of your car, who should be able to advise you on suitable gear ratios for a particular purpose. If this is not possible, and you have to work it out for yourself while testing, keep an accurate note of which gear pulled what revs at which corner. Then, if you go to a new circuit and no one knows, or will tell you, which ratios to use, you can use the data you collected at the earlier circuit if the two tracks seem to be somewhat similar in speed and type of corner. At worst, it should enable you to arrive at the circuit for your first practice with ratios that are not too wildly out.

If, as is likely to be the case, you have only a restricted assortment of alternative ratios, and you cannot get things quite right, at least make sure that you are not pulling too many revs on the straight (better to pull too few than too many), and also try to ensure that you have gears that are right for the corners. If the circuit has a long straight then the corner leading into it is the most important one because if you are slow out of this one you will be slow all the way down the straight that follows.

Tyres are a vital part of racing, so you should take steps to become reasonably knowledgeable about them. Get to know the tyre manufacturers' competition people and learn from them. Get them to explain to you about pressures, the effect of tread depths, and how much you need for drainage in the wet (this is vitally important if you race in a category for which a specific tyre is mandatory). Don't forget that if you are using worn tyres to get a quick time you will use slightly higher revs with less rubber.

While sorting out your suspension, gearing, and tyres you should have come to know your brakes pretty well. Keep a log of the pad wear, and if in doubt about when to change pads, play safe and do the job early. Pad changes don't get any easier if the back plates are welded to the discs.

You should get a rough idea of the fuel consumption of your car, and obviously you should know the precise tank capacity. Check your consumption on fast laps, not running-in ones. Before you finish practising, do a few laps with a full load of fuel, or at least the load you will be carrying at the start of the race, but don't wear out the car testing; there comes a time when you have to get your backside in gear and race the thing. The prolonged test sessions some drivers undertake become a form of neurosis. Bear in mind that you may be one of the people who go quicker in a race when the adrenalin is flowing more freely as a result of the competition around you.

One final point about testing; *don't* experiment afterwards. Repeat: don't experiment after the last test run because, however trivial a change, you may then spend most of your first official practice session trying to solve a secondary fault that has been triggered.

If you know you are going to be racing at a new circuit, at least try to get round it beforehand in a saloon, or if all else fails, on foot. Bear in mind, though, that the corners may then look a lot different when you hit them at speed in a low-slung racing car.

Before practising at a race meeting you have to go through the signing-on and scrutineering formalities, which means having your licence and perhaps homologation forms with you, as well as your record card if you are collecting signatures for a higher graded licence.

Arrive early; try to be the first to be scrutineered, and if the weather looks to be in the least changeable, make sure you are first in the queue for the track, ready to go out the moment practice begins for your event. If it rains halfway through practice, or if it rains after the first two minutes and you've already managed to set a reasonable time in the dry, no one will better it once the track becomes wet. Conversely, without a 'dry' time, you will have to start the race with the serious disadvantage of being at the back of the grid.

Some drivers seem to shy away and hide in the pits if it is wet in practice, but sooner or later you are going to have to race in the rain, and the more practice you've had in it the better. If nothing else, you should be able to test rain tyres. Use one gear higher than normal in the wet and don't put power on until you are exiting a

Probably no one really likes *racing in the wet, but you need to know how to cope. Remember that an electrifying performance in the wet will very definitely get you noticed by team managers.*

corner and the car is straight.

Get the brakes and tyres warmed up before you go for a quick lap under kinder conditions and, if you get a chance midst all the action, try to consider where there will be a moment on each lap where you can glance at your instruments and maybe even find time for breathing exercises to relax you.

Before you start a race, throw away any chewing gum and take out your false teeth; ideally, try not to step in any oil just before getting into the car, otherwise your feet may slip on the pedals. As a final gesture of friendliness, if there is a serious opponent in the race walk up to him and ask for his autograph; he will spend the first couple of laps puzzling about your motives.

When let loose on the warming-up lap (or laps) before a race do them quickly in order to get the car, the tyres, and yourself warmed into race condition. Consider a practice start or two, but don't burn out your clutch, and obviously keep a wary eye in your mirrors before experimenting.

When you finally line up for a start, get someone to rub their hands round your wheels to wipe off any gravel and check the tyres, and then wipe gravel from in front of your start position. Some people have been known to send mechanics with brooms to brush the first half of the circuit in front of the line of their particular car, but this is more to unnerve the opposition than to win races. Bear in mind there will be a lot of noise at the start of a race—take care not to over-rev your engine simply because you

Try to find time to study the start procedure for a race before yours.

can't hear it. If you are starting way down the grid because of a problem in practice, consider which of the cars ahead are likely to be easiest to overtake and which drivers are known to need a disproportionate amount of road.

If the start is downhill, a small stone chock may help to hold the car. Be quite clear about the start procedure being used for your race. It is most important to know the rules precisely because if you jump the start you will be penalized, which will usually put you out of contention (as you will be if you aren't clear about the rules regarding pace cars if used). Above all study the starter's antics in previous races; if he scratches his backside as a nervous reaction just before changing the lights to green, consider going on the scratch.

Know the rules for your event about push starts too. If your engine stalls on the grid, throw one hand in the air, cross yourself with the other, and sit there watching your life flash before your very eyes.

Once under way, your concentration on your own performance should not stop you being aware of what is happening in the race as a whole; you need to cultivate the knack of being aware and 'reading' a race, knowing if someone is charging through the field or whether you are likely to lap people (you should be so lucky), and so on.

Any fool can go fast in a straight line, but cornering is really what it's all about. Basically, you have to decide whether your car understeers or oversteers. Depending on this, you can decide how to enter and exit corners, providing that you have a car that makes up its mind on one attitude.

With an oversteering car you have to get it well round a corner before you can start to accelerate away, while with an understeering car you have to go in a bit slower because it usually doesn't want to turn into a corner, although once it is going round the corner it is much easier to feed the power on because it gives you a better idea of what it is going to do.

Your cornering technique will not only be influenced by the handling of the car but also by what type of car it is. The basic difference between saloons and single-seaters (with sports cars slotted in the middle) is that a single-seater should be ultra-precise. It will change direction without any major discomfort, all the loading, the low centre of gravity, and the confinement of most of the weight so far inboard of the wheels ensuring that there is no great rush of load from one corner to another. With a sports car you may get a certain deadness, the fuel tanks may be out on the edge of the car, and consequently it may not feel quite so precise. This deadness is more exaggerated in a saloon, where you have a high weight as well, so that with the weight of the body the car doesn't react so quickly.

The important thing is to be *very careful on the entry* to a corner because this is the most important part. The last of the late brakers is a dying breed because a car becomes unsettled if you leave things to the last moment and then jump on everything. If you turn in as the car is either right down on its haunches or leaping back up, it is unstable and unbalanced and the weight transfer hasn't had a chance to settle. Better to brake a little bit earlier and more gently, and have the car balanced as you turn in; that way you get the mass going in as a *stable unit*, not literally as a see-saw which never settles through the corner. In short there will be times when 'faster may be slower' and it is better to under- rather than over-drive.

If you have a car that can't make up its mind what it wants to do, then you have to stop planning too far ahead and just basically drive on your reactions, sorting things out as you go through a corner. Really, reactions are more important than theory, and the immaculate textbook lines often have to be thrown out of the window, particularly in race traffic, and especially if you happen to be a genius. Go and watch some of the really quick people—they sometimes establish their own guidelines as they go along. However, bear in mind that if you are unconventional, going through a corner sideways can clobber your exit speed, and speed is something you need to hang on to, particularly with a basically slow car; it will also overheat your tyres. Stand on corners during other races and watch the quick people, using a stopwatch to

Above and below *Overtaking may be easier when the field has spread out and you can pick people off one at a time, but if you dally too long at the start and get overtaken by chargers you will just make extra work for yourself.*

prove the evidence of your own eyes. Don't forget that the handling of a car may change during a race as the fuel load lightens.

Overtaking cannot be practised at test sessions, so this is an art you must perfect during races. Before you get too dynamic you need to know the calibre of your opponents (which is why Grand Prix drivers are rightly nervous of inexperienced people in Formula 1); be aware of other drivers and their skills. Know who you can trust, who are the rock-apes who will take you off, and remember that there will be experienced observers with their eyes on you; if you are over-exuberant on your own you may only injure yourself, but if you are stupid when overtaking you may well hurt

If you run close behind another car you should get a tow to help you make a positive passing manoeuvre.

someone else. As you may if *you* are the one who causes an accident when being overtaken. Mirrors are to see behind with, so use them for that, and remember that while 'using your proper share of the track' is a legitimate way of keeping a key rival in his place, deliberately blocking people who are clearly faster is all rather stupid.

As well as skilled overtaking, cornering, and general racemanship, you can gain some benefit from slipstreaming, particularly on fast circuits as well as those where there are trees that can create a sort of tunnel, giving a bigger tow effect that you obtain in the wide open spaces of somewhere like Silverstone. If you imagine that you are powering through a mass of air, all you are doing when slipstreaming is getting someone else to do the tunnelling so that you can pull up behind them with little or no resistance. The closer you get the better it is, and there is a great deal to be gained from it, particularly in practice where a quick car can tow a team-mate higher up the grid. In such a case you need to sit down and work out carefully how and where you are going to work together.

If you have no team-mate but can see one of the quick boys out

Don't stop concentrating entirely just because you've taken the chequered flag. On rallies in particular, the ends of special stages can be quite dangerous.

on the circuit, slip out ahead of him, wait until he passes you and then try to tuck behind him. Once you've learnt the art you'll almost be able to 'hear' the slipstream because you will feel very slight buffeting in the turbulent air, and you can pick up the exhaust note of the other car in that air. If there is a crosswind you sometimes need to drive not exactly behind the other car, but slightly to one side; if you zig-zag a little you will feel the turbulence on your helmet and will know that you are in the slipstream. A tow can certainly help you to a quick lap time, but on high-speed circuits it is not an activity for the faint-hearted. Also, remember that if you gear your car for a tow and then lose it you may be slower than normal when you are on your own.

Whatever methods you use, aim to win as slowly as possible. The most important people at a race meeting are the spectators; they go to watch races, not walkovers, and 10 per cent of prize money should perhaps be docked from a winner for every second by which he wins.

If and when you take the chequered flag, don't relax too much on your cooling down lap, otherwise you will lose concentration and do something silly. And stay on the correct line, or else your hot tyres may pick up rubbish which you can do without.

You will learn one hell of a lot during your first race, and so the message is obvious: do as much racing as possible. Apart from competition giving you an edge, sheer driving experience is part of your job, even if it's on a push bike or kart. The occasional trip to a skid pan may keep an edge on your sense of balance too.

If, in order to gain as much experience as possible, you decide to enter for more than one race at a race meeting, try to make sure that they are not consecutive events, or life will become too hectic for intelligent planning, or for you to learn by your activities. And you must learn something from every race if you are to climb the ladder.

One important thing as you struggle upwards: learn to stay sane and in control of your emotions during a race. Some of the Desperate Dan tactics one sees—even in F1—should earn the drivers suspension for life. If people want trophies so badly they should go to a jewellers and buy some.

Below *are the forces enacted by simple braking and acceleration. The more forceful either operation, the more exaggerated the lift and pitch, and therefore the more distortion of the tyres' contact patch or reduction of the pressure of the tyres on the road.*

Right *shows what happens to your strut/shock absorber under such forces*

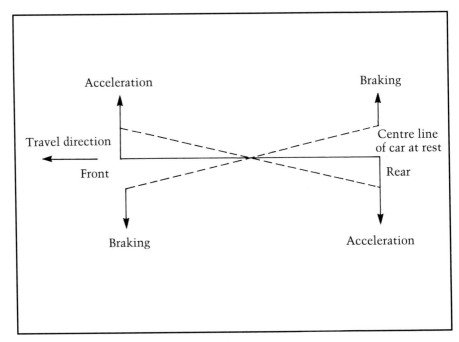

FRONT STRUT

At Rest   Braking   Acceleration

Bump rubber

Free travel suspension movement

No free suspension travel left

REAR SHOCK ABSORBER

At Rest   Acceleration   Braking

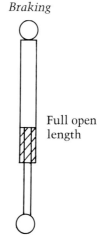

Full open length

Free travel

If exaggerated, starts to pick up wheel off ground

Normal suspension movements
For rally car 5"-6"
$2^1/_2$-3" of bump from ride
$2^1/_2$-3" of droop from ride

For race car FF 1600

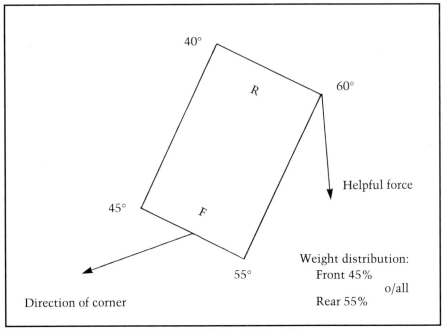

Above *Optimum cornering force: (i) if balance is right . . .*

Below *. . . (ii) if balance is wrong:*

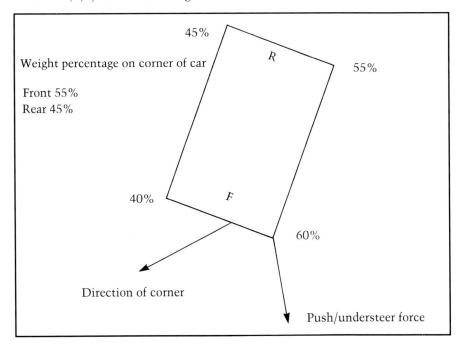

Above *Perfect balance as shown in the diagram opposite.*

Below *Same corner, same car but with violent understeer and the car trying to push out as illustrated opposite.*

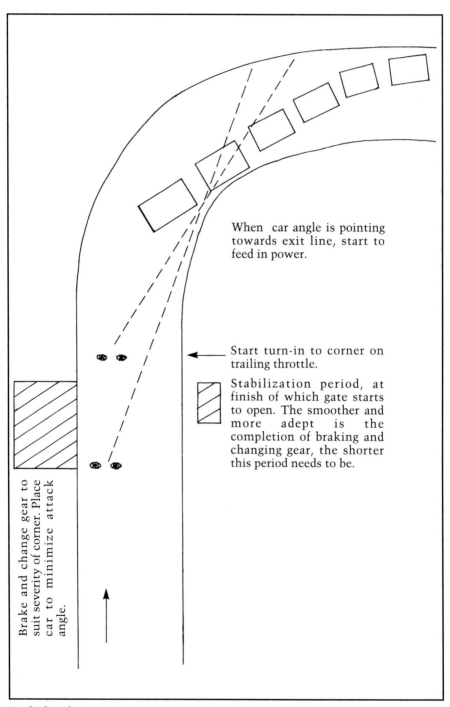

When car angle is pointing towards exit line, start to feed in power.

Start turn-in to corner on trailing throttle.

Stabilization period, at finish of which gate starts to open. The smoother and more adept is the completion of braking and changing gear, the shorter this period needs to be.

Brake and change gear to suit severity of corner. Place car to minimize attack angle.

Right-hand corner

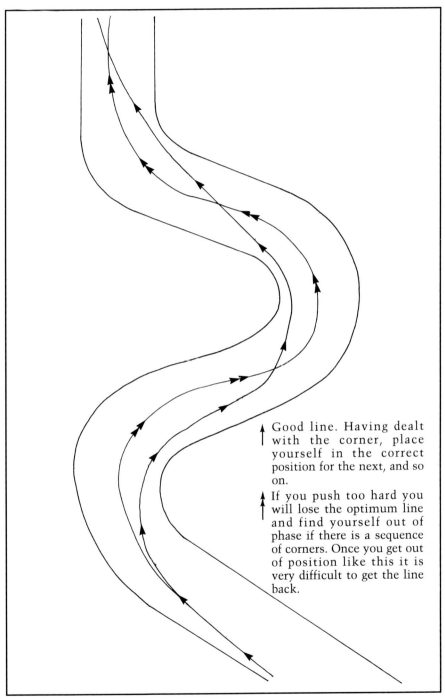

Good line. Having dealt with the corner, place yourself in the correct position for the next, and so on.

If you push too hard you will lose the optimum line and find yourself out of phase if there is a sequence of corners. Once you get out of position like this it is very difficult to get the line back.

S-bend

This page and opposite *In this sequence, the positioning of the car is very good, but the driver has used too much oversteer and therefore has to use too much opposite lock to balance it. This acts like a brake and prevents optimum forward movement. Compare the photograph on p. 105.*

9

On Stage

Having prepared your rally car, you will doubtless be agog to start an event to demonstrate the talent with which you are undoubtedly brimming. However, although you may not wish to share the glory, you have to recognize that in rallying a *co-driver* is a fairly important animal so choose him (or her) with care. Above all, will you and your co-driver be compatible? You don't *have* to have the same likes, dislikes, interests or hobbies, in fact some rally crews have worked well when the two in the cabin have hardly spoken to one another; but it is more enjoyable if you and your co-driver do get on together. Does his rallying background complement yours? Has he got wide experience? Can he get adequate time off work to complete your programme? What will be the split of expenses and, touch wood, winnings? If he smokes and you are a non-smoker, should you find someone else? Do his feet smell or does he suffer from flatulence? Will this bother you? If so maybe you need to look for somebody else. Does he show signs of wanting to be a press-on hero driver himself? Goodbye. Obviously, if you have a choice of co-drivers and their skills are roughly equal, choose the lighter one.

You and your co-driver will perform better if you get yourself properly organized before an event: know who is doing what, who is looking after entries, licences, hotel bookings, and so on. Develop a checklist so that you don't forget anything; include all the things you will need for driving—overalls, underwear, shoes, gloves, and helmet (with an appropriately valid sticker on it). And have a spare key for the car.

It will help build confidence if you develop a routine before rallies. For instance, check your intercom the night before and make sure you have a spare battery and that the co-driver knows where it is. Check the car for rattles, loose articles left in it by mistake—spanners or nuts and bolts that could roll around and get underneath your feet on a stage—in other words, anything that can distract or even be dangerous. Make sure that the horn, lights, etc all work so that the car will pass scrutineering without any problem, because if you are failed by the scrutineer and have to make last minute changes to comply, it will all increase your anxiety and reduce your effectiveness.

Practise wheel changes with your co-driver before an event, correction: before *every* event. Yes, it's a chore but if you don't do it you will get rusty; each of you must know his exact part in the proceedings.

Think through and plan an event together so that you and your co-driver agree that if you have a puncture with, say, six miles to go you will stop and change it if it's a rear wheel puncture; if it's a *front* wheel puncture you will stop to change it even if you've only a couple of miles to go.

You often see athletes talking to themselves before a race, working through where they are hoping to be at particular stages; you should do something similar. For example, discuss your objectives for the rally you are about to tackle. Are you there just for driving experience? If so your objective is to cover as many miles as possible, and improving your technique and learning may be as important as sheer speed. Are you in a championship and need to accumulate points, or are you going for an outright win? *Plan* your attack on the rally with these things in mind. Study the results pattern of previous events—does the leader on Day 1 ever lead at the end or always break?

If you know the condition of all the stages, discuss whether to try harder on the smoother stages, saving the car on the rougher ones, or whether to risk trying hard from the start; if smooth stages come first it's probably worth trying to build a lead on them so that the others break their cars trying to catch you on the later rougher stages. Ideally, you shouldn't be aiming to go flat out until you've got into a rhythm. Have an outline plan of attack; try to stick to it and don't get sidetracked by competitors who may try to out-psyche you. All with the rider, of course, that if something unusual happens then you must be flexible enough to seize opportunities; as an extreme example, if your aim is to finish sixth or seventh and the top five drivers drop out, then you should tear up your plan and try hard to beat the bloke you were fighting for sixth place because now you have an unexpected chance of an outright win.

You don't need to make yourself neurotic by considering every contingency, but if you have thought things through quietly and calmly away from the pressure of a rally then you will be that

Present a rally car at scrutineering at the right time and with the right documentation.

much better able to cope, and will save precious seconds, if you hit a problem.

You will help yourself keep calm if you allow adequate time to get to the starting point. If you are staying overnight don't go to bed unreasonably early because you just won't sleep; equally, don't spend a late night out on the town even if it is the first place you've stayed in with traffic lights and Chinese take-away. Report to scrutineering at your nominated time with the car looking clean, and if the press are there make yourself known to them. When you reach the giddy heights that the public are actually interested in you (you will, you will), then find time to sign autographs and talk to people. You are in showbusiness and have a public to please, so behave accordingly; the fact that too many F1 drivers act as boorish prima donnas is no reason for you to do the same. Whether you chat with other competitors at scrutineering and when signing on, or remain aloof in an attempt (probably forlorn) to psyche them, is entirely up to you; different folks have different strokes.

The co-driver will probably be looking after the pure administration of the car, and once the rally starts (and once it does, by the way, many of your nerves will disappear) it will be his job to direct you gently to the first special section. Keep in mind that rallying isn't everyone's cup of tea and don't hand opponents ammunition by driving like a hooligan on public roads.

Preparation and planning in advance are important, but rallies are won or lost on special stages and these need your maximum concentration. When you enter the stage start control, your co-driver will check you in and you will normally have one minute to move up to the actual start line. If possible, watch the previous competitor start: note the start procedure, how much wheel spin he gets and where his wheels were placed. On a gravel stage there will probably be two deep grooves dug in the road: consider where the maximum traction is likely to be gained and position your car accordingly as you drive on to the start line.

As you are given the start signal (and you must of course have carefully checked what the procedure is in advance) and you drop the clutch, remember that wheel spin—while all very dramatic—is actually slower than a more controlled attack. If the wheels spin the car will probably slide from side to side, which is also inefficient. If a start area is very slippery it may pay to start in second gear to avoid wheelspin.

Having moved away from the start line with as little aggravation as possible, the next thing you will have to do is engage a higher gear. Remember, if it is a synchromesh gear box, make it nice and smooth and DO NOT HURRY the change. And incidentally, you shouldn't be driving at 100 per cent at this early stage in your career; drive at 80 per cent maximum. Engage the next gears as necessary; then eventually it is highly likely that you will come to a corner, which—like it or not—will unstabilize the car; it will unstabilize you too if you don't *assess* the corner

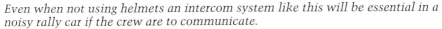

Even when not using helmets an intercom system like this will be essential in a noisy rally car if the crew are to communicate.

Above and below *A rally crew must be absolutely clear about the procedure at the start of special stages and should try to watch an earlier car start if possible. Note the tulip arrows in the co-driver's road book.*

properly. One way of assessing the degree of severity of a corner is to compare the farthest point you can see on the inside of the corner with the farthest point you can see on the outside of it. The closer those two points look the tighter the bend is; the greater the distance between them, the less severe the corner. Judging corners like this will come with experience and, obviously, the more you drive the more you will be able to assess terrain and feel whether roads are going to do something nasty. Assessing corners should of course be easy if your co-driver is calling over pace notes for a section you've practised in advance.

When cornering, try to use a racing line for smoothness; for instance, if a bend goes to the right, try to position yourself as far to the left as you reasonably can—without putting the car in the ditch of course. Place the car where the surface is firm, too, so that you have the maximum grip under braking because, having assessed the severity of the corner, you need to reduce speed and select the correct gear in which to take it. You should be aiming to have completed your de-acceleration process and allowed the car's suspension to stabilize *before* you turn in. You then turn the car into the corner from the outside clipping point towards the inside

Not an example of how to save tyre wear on a Subaru but a fine driver (Markku Alen) in full cry.

apex point, on a trailing throttle and ideally with the suspension in the middle of its travel.

Obviously, corners are where rallies are won or lost, so let us consider them according to the different types of car you may be using. First, the 'old' front-engine, rear-wheel drive cars that are the one exception to the point about taking a smooth racing line. With these, use what is called a pendulum action, first kicking the tail towards the inside of the corner, then to the outside, driving through the corner in a constant state of over-steer. This technique is why such cars are so popular with spectators. And don't win top rallies nowadays.

Now front-wheel drive cars. With these you should be seeking to use as little lock as possible, because for every degree of lock over roughly five degrees, you lose steering efficiency. You should be trying to have the back of the car sliding so that the front wheels point to the apex and the car goes round in a drift with the front wheels pointing in the direction you are aiming.

Finally, today's winners, the four-wheel drive cars. Be as neutral as possible with these because you've got all four wheels working for you. Concentrate on the line and allow the traction and grip that the car has to hold it on line. Over-steer or under-steer creates friction—you've got enough of this with four-wheel drive anyway without putting more into it by getting the car off line. So no fireworks.

It is always better to be slow in and fast out of corners. By going

Left-foot braking is an asset only if you get it right, so practise before rallies

in a bit slower, you will be more in control of the situation, and by accelerating smoothly all the way through the corner you will come to the next straight that much faster. Exciting isn't it?

Always try to *brake* in a straight line, and on rough rallies remember that if you brake hard when there are potholes, you will close the front suspension up so that the car has no suspension travel left and you are likely to bounce and jump all over the road; always try to leave some suspension for driving over hazards. Incidentally, the much talked about technique of left foot braking was started by the Scandinavians in Saabs and Minis where there is no drive to the rear. By using the left foot on the brake pedal (and hence usually changing gear without using the clutch) they found they could 'balance' the car by playing the brake and accelerator pedals. The power you apply by using the right pedal 'fights' the brakes and keeps the front wheels working and pulling; but the rear brakes work and settle the back of the car so that you can get it to slide slightly out of line, in a drift situation with the front wheels still merrily pulling you along. You don't need brutal application of the brakes but the technique does need practice. If you try it, find somewhere quiet and loose to do so, and if you find yourself getting into hopeless tangles then abandon the idea.

Instead of left-foot braking, you may use the handbrake to lock the rear wheels and slide the rear of the car out of line, but remember to de-clutch if you do this on rear-wheel drive cars.

If you encounter wet roads (as you will) or snow and ice, the driving techniques are really the same except it may be more difficult to assess the amount of grip you've got in some conditions than others; black ice, often where water has thawed and then re-frozen, can be particularly difficult to judge and treacherous. Ideally, in such conditions have the car in more of an over-steer situation, certainly on the entrance to corners. The same applies to a blind rally where you don't know which way the roads go; it is preferable to have the car in a state of controlled over-steer. However, if you are using pace notes, whether on gravel, tarmac, or wet, then look for the cleanest racing line; you don't need the car to be unbalanced.

One thing to remember on cornering techniques: if friends or spectators say 'You were spectacular' the chances are you weren't going very quickly. A smooth efficient line is more important than playing to the crowds.

Moving on, if you successfully negotiate all the straights and corners you will eventually come to the end of the stage, where you may well have a flying finish. Care! Obviously you don't want to lose time by braking *before* the flying finish, and there *should* be enough road for you to come to a halt at the stop control.

However, an absurd number of accidents happen at the end of special sections, through drivers being so relieved that they've got to the end that they lose concentration, or through organizers allowing inadequate stopping distance, or through spectators getting in the way. So concentrate as hard at the end of a stage as you did over the rest of it.

Not all stages go smoothly and apart from problems at the finish you may encounter other variables:

- *Hazard signs* erected by organizers, especially on blind events. Take note of them. One would think it needed special training in idiocy to have accidents at places that have been specially indicated by organizers, but it happens. Just don't let it happen to you.

- *Yumps,* which is what the English patronizingly assume Scandinavians call jumps because they can't pronounce 'j'. Forget the flying cars on videos; *minimize* the time spent in the air because when you are airborne you've got no acceleration (the wheels haven't got a lot to grip on have they?). In addition, you've no braking or steering and if you continually fly flat out over yumps, eventually you will hit a big one and may do a lot of damage to the car when you land. Worse, if the road goes left or right, while you are up there trying to get your pilot's licence, when you land you will be an accident looking for somewhere to park.

Rally cars jumping make a marvellous sight but flying can sometimes be slower and more car damaging than a gentler approach.

Incidentally, some drivers apply a quick dab with the left foot on the brake to bring the nose down before going over a brow so that the car doesn't fly too high. Avoid hard braking as you land by the way—you will need all the suspension travel to absorb the landing without compressing it by braking. (Ignore this advice if the roadmaker has been churlish enough to put a T junction over a blind brow.)

- *Water.* If you approach water too fast you are likely to aquaplane and, as with flying over brows, the car is in control of you, *you* aren't in control of *it.* However careful your car preparation, if you hit water *too* hard it may well flood everything and possibly stop the engine; even worse you may take on water through the intake system and actually seize the engine. So . . . be a bit gentle.

- *Night-driving.* You probably won't have to do much of this but if it is likely, perhaps through a rally running late, then make sure before the event that your lights all work and are properly set up. Set them up with the car in rally trim with the crew on board so that the height is adjusted; you don't want your lights pointing at the sky. What you do want is a nice spread of lights so that you can see not only straight ahead but also left and right up to an angle of about 25°. If your extra lights are being carried on board a service vehicle be sure to fit them well before it gets dark—you will be at a

If you charge into water on a rally you may stall and perhaps do even more damage. Caution is recommended.

disadvantage if you are forced to drive on only standard headlights.

- *Fog.* Not nice. Proper lighting may help—diffusers over the top of the lights will stop glare back onto the screen, for instance—or if it's a blind event even try turning off all the lights and driving on the shadows. To some extent driving in fog is a matter of confidence; if you start to think about what you are actually doing, you may slow to a crawl. You may find it more relaxing, particularly on road sections, to follow other competitors, but be careful that you don't then find that you've followed the district nurse into the drive of her cottage.

  One technique worth considering for driving in fog is to use one gear higher than you think you ought to be in. If you have a lower gear, and are on and off the throttle and abrupt with the steering, you will think that you are driving very rapidly because of all the action going on as you get into a sweat. In fact all that is inefficient; it's better and quicker to go up that gear and to try to do everything smoothly.

- *Dust* can be as frustrating as fog and it will probably make you cough more if the car isn't adequately sealed against it. If dust is hanging in the air because there is no wind, then accept that it is the same for everyone (except the lucky devil running first on the road). If dust is thrown up by other cars, as it invariably is on the Safari, it becomes important not to waste time at service points, thus allowing other cars to overtake you.

  It will be difficult to overtake in dust; in fact unless the other driver is aware of you it can be difficult on any special stage. Flash your lights, blow your horn, but keep yourself under control—don't ram him or lose your temper because you may go off in your anger. Don't baulk other people by the way; crass behaviour.

- Sooner or later you will have a *puncture.* If you and the co-driver have practised and worked out who does what, then you will be that much more efficient in changing a wheel. It is up to the co-driver to know exactly where you are on the stage so that you can make an instant decision on whether to stop or limp on with the flat.

If you are trying really hard and hoping to reach the top, then sooner or later you may hit a more serious problem and go off the road and crash. We are *not* recommending that you crash but top drivers almost seem to display a skill in the way in which they

Above and below *If dust is hanging around on rallies because there is no wind to blow it away, console yourself with the thought that it's the same for everyone except the first car. The aerials on these cars are not for picking up the BBC World Service but for inter-team radio communications.*

actually have accidents. If there are three trees and one looks more likely to bend, that's the one the top driver is likely to hit; the more mundane driver may clout a stouter one which puts him out of the rally. The better the driver the longer he is likely to stay (roughly) in control of a situation. One of the authors rolled down the side of a hill with Eric Carlsson and while the car was rolling Carlsson had the wit to switch off so that no petrol was pumping when the crash ended. Roger Clark maintains that if all else is lost and you know you are going off you should dip the clutch and apply full throttle so that when rescuers find the remains they will see 11,000 on the rev counter and say 'Ye gods, he was going.' You may not wish to go to such extremes but if you feel you are going off, *don't* just shut your eyes. Try to stay in control and, for instance, if the engine and radiator are at the front of the car try to absorb any impact with the back of the car, because you are more likely to stay in the rally.

Having had an accident, try to remain calm and assess the situation. The most important thing may be simply to protect where you are by sending someone up the road to warn the next

If you need spectator assistance on a rally, it will help if the co-driver is decisive and organizes things so that people are pushing or pulling in the same direction.

Above and below *Spectator control is a continuing problem for rallies because even when moved by marshals, people will often persist in returning to dangerous points. If you want to reach the top you must steel yourself to press on in these conditions.*

car, otherwise the accident may get worse. Think calmly and consider the best way to regain the road. Utilize any spectators who appear—as they probably will, even in the most deserted parts of the Safari Rally—to the maximum. It's better for someone to say '3,2,1, *lift*' so that everybody works together rather than have people pushing and pulling in different directions. Incidentally, on the Safari Rally and in other remote places, you will find that coins or notes will help the lifting process, so carry some.

When you have spectators and/or marshals organized to push or pull you out of a ditch or bog, have all the wheels on the car as straight as possible. If you've gone off with a lot of lock on the wheels and try to move the car with it still applied you will just be making heavy weather of things.

By the way, if you have an accident don't attempt to bluff or tell lies to your team about what happened. Engineers won't learn anything if they are fed duff information, and in any case it is almost inevitable nowadays that someone will roll up afterwards with amateur video shots of you making a porridge of things.

We don't want to give you the impression that special stages all have problems, although to continue the litany we must mention that from time to time you may find yourself faced with the problem of driving at speed close to *spectators*. Hard though it may seem, you've got to try to forget about them, although you

Below left and this page *Rally service points are interesting for spectators and vital for competitors. On Safari Rallies they become pit stops because if someone passes while you are stopped, you may have to follow his dust for miles.*

should be alert enough to notice if all spectators are looking skywards; it may be that they've been distracted by, say, a filming helicopter and haven't heard you coming. If you note that spectators aren't looking at you but down the road in the direction you are heading it may mean that someone has had an accident. Again, be alert. If spectators are standing on a stage you have practised and have pace notes for, remember they may put you off by standing on your line, so that the corner doesn't look the same as it did on your recce. In popular places, like the top of the Turini on the Monte Carlo Rally, the sheer volume of spectators will change the shape of the road, especially if police erect control barriers.

You've sweated over the special stage, you've got to the finish control, you've coped with all the hazards; now let us assume you arrive at a service point. You should discuss what work needs doing with your co-driver and he should list it in order of priority. If the exhaust is falling of or you've got a puncture, people will not be pleased if you first get them to attend to the little holder you have for your cough drops. If you have radio communication the co-driver should tell your service crew what needs doing in advance. If you are not in radio contact then *one* person in the rally car should brief *one* member of any support crew—a general shouting match will just cause confusion. Know exactly how much time you have at service points, and do be realistic. If you've got 10 minutes *don't* play safe and tell the mechanics that you've only got 5 because that will mean that an 8-minute job will not be done. Get into the habit of running through a mental checklist as you leave a service point—check brake pedal pressure; bonnet catches secure; steering wheel alignment corect; gauges working, and so on.

At rest halts be sure that your co-driver and/or service crew know exactly where you are before you wander off to chat to the press, get food, or whatever. If the halt is a parc fermé with cars parked for some time, remember to isolate the electrics; many drivers have been penalized because their cars wouldn't start under their own power because of something left switched on.

Whether you can sleep or not at halts will entirely depend on your own particular make-up. You are more likely to sleep if you feel relaxed and confident—in other words, if you've thought through the event, know what you are doing, have confidence in your co-driver and in your service support. You will become even more confident if you have the ability to learn by experience—for example, after a stage try to find time to jot down how it went, any mistakes you made, plus information that will help you to drive better if you do the stage again. Apart from anything else it will

Rallycross provides good driving experience for rallying although it is unlikely to get you noticed by any of the works rally teams.

make comparisons of your stage times with your rivals more valid afterwards. It follows of course that you need to know if key rivals had, say, punctures on a stage where you appear to have murdered them. If you have a good working relationship with your co-driver ask him how he thinks you drove on the stage; you may even be able to tell by the colour of his knuckles. Some drivers even give themselves marks for their braking, throttle control, gearchanging, etc on special stages. You may not wish to go to these lengths but can we at least encourage you to THINK about your driving.

Let us end the chapter with a brief look at *rallycross*, which can be useful training for rallying. As the surfaces are a mixture of gravel and tarmac it's all very good practice and it would certainly be better to do a rallycross at a weekend than sit at home if there's no rally. There will be four or five other cars around you but as you are going round a known piece of road, you can concentrate on line and length and on getting the balance of the car right. Get someone to time every lap—or even particular sections—so that you can see if your technique is improving.

But a word of caution—don't expect rallycross to lead you to rally stardom. At the time of writing, rallycross has something of a gypsy image and is not really seen as a breeding ground by team managers. However, if environmental pressures crowd in on rallying itself, then the authors believe that rallycross is potentially a star sport simply waiting to be properly promoted.

10

Co-Driving

Though a less glamorous route than driving it is possible to climb fairly high in motorsport as a rally *co-driver*. This person, who can be of either sex, used simply to pore over the maps, plot references, and then direct the driver to the right point. Nowadays he is likely to be much more of a business manager, not necessarily the brain but certainly the nerve centre for the administration of a rally car. He also needs to be something of a psychologist to get the best out of a driver—it is his job to notice if the driver's eyes have started to come out on stalks, which is usually an indication that it is time to calm things if the car is to stay on the road.

The exact role of the co-driver depends to some extent on how involved the driver himself wants to be but, broadly, the co-driver's job is to present both car and driver to special stage starts in the best possible condition. As such he can't win an event but he can most certainly lose one; a co-driver therefore needs to be disciplined, organized, compatible, and able to cope with tantrums (by his driver and perhaps officials). He mustn't panic and he mustn't have an ego, because the driver will probably have one large enough for the whole crew and will want to take any glory. Sometimes a co-driver even needs to be something of a bluffer, bluffing officials over timing or, not least, his own driver so that he doesn't lose confidence if the co-driver has made a mistake; the driver may lack confidence in his own abilities and can do without worrying about the co-driver's capabilities too.

Background? Well, co-drivers used to come from road rallies where the tasks of ploting and accurate map-reading seemed to instil the right discipline, and many drivers today regret that this is no longer the case. Nowadays they arrive through a variety of routes and if you want to make your way as one then, as with the driver, start by eating, sleeping, and reading rallying. Helping to

Co-drivers have been around for years — this shot from the Paris-Madrid in 1903 makes it look as if they once used their feet for extra braking.

organize events won't be bad experience either.

As far as equipment is concerned, your capital outlay will be much less than your driver's—you will simply need pens, pencils, maps, etc. You will probably overload yourself with too much gimicky equipment (as a psychological crutch) at first and then cut back later, but when buying items get the best and keep up to date; if you are using an abacus and everyone else has a pocket calculator, you may appear slightly out of touch.

Do keep in mind when getting equipment that sharp or hard objects flying about in a car can be dangerous; more than one co-driver has broken a pelvis through a hard mapboard jamming between their stomach and the dashboard.

Should you carry a camera? On a recce, yes, as we will cover later; but on a rally *no* because of the unnecessary weight. A lightweight in-car television camera, which will gain the team and its sponsors publicity, is a different matter.

You must have the latest *maps* and they shouldn't be tattered and torn otherwise you may find yourself trying to navigate down a crease in one of them. Colour photostats may be appropriate, for instance for particular service areas; the legality of using these must be between you and your conscience. You may need small-scale maps for general route and service plotting, plus large-scale maps for special stages. Use a specialist map supplier rather than your local stationer because you need to cultivate a relationship with someone who is aware of what is happening in the world of maps so that you always have the latest ones.

Moving on from maps, *documentation* is a key element of the co-driver's function as office manager. Again, depending on how

Co-drivers should establish a link with a specialist map supplier so that they always have the latest editions.

involved the driver wishes to be, or whether the crew is driving for a works or supported team, it will probably be the co-driver's job to obtain the rally regulations. These should be read and fully understood with any points queried before events start and, if serious enough, even before entries are made. It may well be the

Essential reading for rally crews. Co-drivers should watch for amendments or bulletins with additional information.

co-driver's job to make the entry, obtain the proper licences, plan travel arrangements, book hotels, liaise with sponsors, draw up a movements schedule, and, not least, plot service. It's a full life.

It will be the co-driver's job to watch for organizers updates, route amendments, and so on; during this stage maintain good relations with rally organizers—don't hector or be too demanding, because you may well need their co-operation and support later. If you have a friendly link they may, for instance, tell you over the 'phone of a possible route change that is likely to come, thus preventing you wasting time in unnecessary reconnaissance. Establish where and when road books will be issued, and where and at what time results should be announced.

Co-drivers working with road books will need to cultivate the ability to read 'tulip arrows'. As the illustration shows, these are a graphic way of indicating which route to take. The name comes from the Tulip Rally where it is believed they were first seen. Clear though they are, a co-driver should still try to get the 'feel' for how an organizer treats junctions when drawing up a tulip road book. At times on rallies you almost need to be able to read an organizer's mind.

As you accumulate equipment and documentation, you will realize that you need pockets or pouches to keep things in, both in your overalls and within the car; develop a habit of keeping things in specific places to save having to fumble around in the heat of an event.

A crew will be more competent on a rally if they know they are likely to meet mechanics at pre-arranged points, and therefore the planning of service is likely to be an important part of a co-driver's job. When drawing up a service plan, you may be the one to have to work out wheel/tyre logistics and you may be the one actually to conduct the service meeting so that everyone knows exactly what their duties are and where they are expected to be at specific times (as well as where they are *not* supposed to be: avoid prohibited areas).

If you have limited resources then plan to maximize what you have. There is a temptation for works teams, not unnaturally perhaps, to put service after every stage with the almost ludicrous result of service after stages only one kilometre long. Frankly, if you and your car can't do at least two kilometres without having a nervous or mechanical breakdown, then you are not going to get very far in a rally. When plotting service, by the way, on no account set excessively demanding schedules. It's too easy to forget that reloading a van at the end of a service point takes time, particularly if the mechanics need a moment to talk over what has just been done to the car and what needs doing next . . . all this can

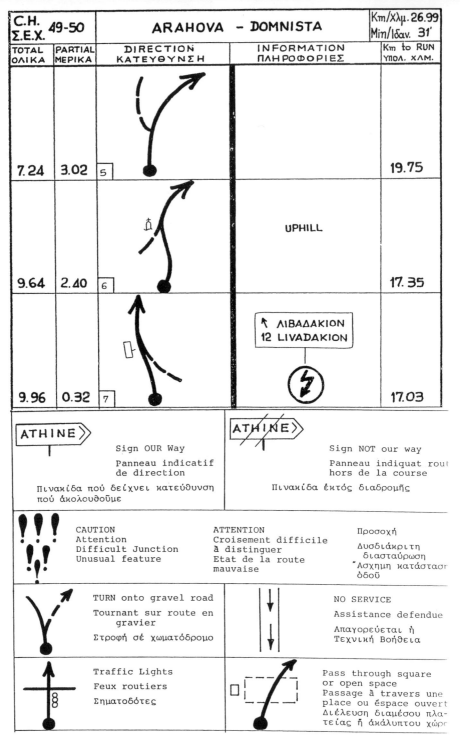

C.H. Σ.Ε.Χ. 49-50		ARAHOVA – DOMNISTA		Km/Χλμ. 26.99 Min/Ιδαν. 31'
TOTAL ΟΛΙΚΑ	PARTIAL ΜΕΡΙΚΑ	DIRECTION ΚΑΤΕΥΘΥΝΣΗ	INFORMATION ΠΛΗΡΟΦΟΡΙΕΣ	Km to RUN ΥΠΟΛ. ΧΛΜ.
7.24	3.02	5		19.75
9.64	2.40	6	UPHILL	17.35
9.96	0.32	7	↖ ΛΙΒΑΔΑΚΙΟΝ 12 LIVADAKION	17.03

ATHINE⟩

Sign OUR Way

Panneau indicatif de direction

Πινακίδα πού δείχνει κατεύθυνση πού ἀκολουθοῦμε

ATHINE⟩

Sign NOT our way

Panneau indiquat rout hors de la course

Πινακίδα ἐκτός διαδρομῆς

CAUTION
Attention
Difficult Junction
Unusual feature

ATTENTION
Croisement difficile à distinguer
Etat de la route mauvaise

Προσοχή
Δυσδιάκριτη διασταύρωση
Ἄσχημη κατάστασι ὁδοῦ

TURN onto gravel road

Tournant sur route en gravier

Στροφή σέ χωματόδρομο

NO SERVICE

Assistance defendue

Απαγορεύεται ἡ Τεχνική Βοήθεια

Traffic Lights

Feux routiers

Σηματοδότες

Pass through square or open space

Passage à travers une place ou éspace ouvert

Διέλευση διαμέσου πλατείας ἤ ἀκάλυπτου χώρι

Tulip arrows provide a very clear way of indicating which road to take. Although a key will be provided, as in the second illustration, on some rallies co-drivers may still need to get a feel for how, for instance, organizers treat minor junctions and so on.

NO	LOCATION	FIRST RALLY CAR	SERVICE CREWS		FROM PREVIOUS POINT			FUEL, TYRES, NOTES
					KMS	TIME	ROUTE	
	ROAD BOOK PAGE 49 REF: 20/21	FRI 26						FUEL 40 Litres
19	BEFORE SS9 / Side road between these junctions / (Possible in hotel road at / Ref 20)	16.45	S5	T5	35	1.30	To Hartola and north on 59. Call at Point 15 on south side of Joutsa for tyres. Continue on 59 and 5kms north of Town L onto 610 and then in 3.5kms L towards Joutsenlampi. This is P49, Ref 21 from opposite direction.	Tyres for SS9
				M1	5	0.10	610 and L in 3.5kms.	SERVICE TIME 8 Mins
	ROAD BOOK PAGE 54 REF: 15							FUEL 0 Litres
20	AFTER SS9 / On 613 100M north of junction at / Post Office / Alt. Houses and lanes from 0.25 / to 3.0kms after Ref 15 going / north	17.20	S8		25	0.40	Not much time! Return on 610 to Kitula and then right onto 613. In about 12kms join Road Book at P 54, Ref 15 and use first side road, etc.	E1 arrive early and find place / Emergency only
				E1	63	1.40	59 to Joutsa, 610 and 613 to service as for S8.	SERVICE TIME (25) Mins
	ROAD BOOK PAGE 60 REF: 44						Return on 59. Call at Point 15 on south side of Jamsa for tyres for SS10 (mixed surface). Continue on 59 and pick up Road Book at Viisarimaki at Junc. 59/613. P55, Ref 19. Follow Road Book to service.	FUEL 15 Litres
21	BEFORE SS10 / In Service Area (at Ice Hall)	18.15	S1 S7	T1	100 115	3.00 3.00		S7 arrive early and get good space / Tyres for SS10 (Mixed Surface?)
				M2	80	1.15	610 and 613 to Viisarimaki and then	M2 try to arrive for 2nd and 3rd cars
			MOTORHOME		75	1.30	R.Book as for S1 & T1	SERVICE TIME 25 Mins

Service schedules should be clear and unambiguous and, where possible, should indicate how much time the rally cars are likely to have in hand.

leave them with dangerously little time to get to their next scheduled point.

Once an event gets underway, a key task—though one that will usually be fairly simple—is to keep the driver on the right route; it is inexcusable to get lost. On road sections tell the driver what he needs to know; it's the co-driver's fault if a car sets off at five-tenths when it should be taken at ten-tenths because of notorious traffic blockages further along the route.

When you get to special stages it will be the co-driver's job to handle control procedures and then to help the driver by using large scale maps (if unpractised) or by calling over *pace notes.* As the name implies, pace notes are simply a way of reminding or advising the driver on what is or isn't going to happen round the next bend, so that he can be both quicker and safer. The co-driver calls the notes out during the stage, and for this he needs good communications via an intercom system, plus a sensitive backside so that he 'feels' where the car is while he is busy with his head down looking at the notes. Obviously, a resistance to car sickness (or at least an ability to ignore it) is a prime requirement for a co-driver.

Pace notes should ideally be made by the crew that will actually be using them on the rally and they should be prepared during

SS1   TRIOS - ESSOS   12 km   Record 8m 37s.

START KM STONE 4.

50   R3   L4 > R3 <   100   HPR

70   L3/c   50   BUMPS   L2   R3

150   R5 BY WHITE POSTS 200   C   100

||| JUMP 50 ! R1

Above *Pace notes make a rally crew both safer and faster. In this example numbers are used to grade the corners.*

Below *The same section of stage but this time in plainer language with E (easy), M (medium), etc used to describe the road. In both illustrations C = crest while symbols underlined are to be read out together. Dotted and solid underlining in different colours can be used to indicate patchy and continuous ice, snow, or gravel. The system doesn't matter so long as it is clear to everyone in the team.*

50   ER   FL > ER <   100   HPR

70   EL/c   50   BUMPS   ML   ER

150   R BY WHITE POSTS 200   C   100

||| JUMP 50 ! HR

several practice runs over a stage. The degree and complexity of the notes depends entirely on the driver and it is important to strike a balance between over- and under-information. Avoid ambiguity in making notes. 'Slight' can easily be confused with 'right', which could be dangerous. Some crews use numbers to grade bends, which they feel leads to crisp communication— 'three' means a bend of a certain severity, for instance. Others use right, left, max, min, or whatever. It doesn't really matter what system is used provided the crew can understand each other. Pace notes are an *aide-mémoire* and should therefore use whatever system suits the driver. However, if the co-driver is unhappy he may tactfully suggest that they have become too elaborate and he can't say it all quickly enough to help the driver. There is a temptation to include too much detail so that you end up with absurdities like 'medium fast right minus maybe' to describe a corner. Watching rallies on television with in-car cameras it is frankly rare to see pace notes being used particularly effectively. Every so often revisit your pace note system and simplify it.

It helps if a team of two or three cars uses the same pace note system, because it may then be possible for co-drivers to exchange notes during reconnaissance to save time. If a team has crews that will be using notes in different languages it helps if at least the key corners appear in the same place on a page so that if people are making ice or gravel notes they can trace the same particular stretch of road on anyone's notes irrespective of the language. Incidentally, *navigational* instructions incorporated in pace notes, that is where you take an actual turning, should be clearly indicated in case for some reason the organizers don't block off the other roads. It is also helpful to include obvious landmarks like kilometre posts, unusual telegraph poles or road signs to help you find your place again in the notes if you get confused.

Ice/gravel notes

Pace notes tell the driver where the road goes next; ice and gravel notes tell him the *condition* of the road—whether it is likely to be loose or have ice or snow on it.

Having such notes not only makes a rally safer but faster, too. Safer because if, say, telegraph poles cut across a corner, the co-driver will be advising the driver that the road in fact doesn't but hairpins to the left or right; safer, too, if he can warn the driver that the road is loose or icy. And faster because blind corners which are in fact fast ones can be taken at the right speed if the co-driver advises accordingly.

Ice and gravel notes help greatly if there's a long special section with just a couple of dodgy sections—the driver will be able to run on racing tyres with the co-driver carefully warning where the slippery sections are.

Ideally, ice and gravel notes should be made as close to the arrival of the rally as possible (tact may be needed in gaining access to stages) and they should be made by someone with rally experience, preferably a recently retired or currently unemployed rally driver with an experienced co-driver. If such a person is not at your disposal, then stress that whoever makes ice/gravel notes for you must be consistent. Such notes should also be realistic; they should not be over-complicated because time may be short at a service point and the rally driver needs to say 'I need this or that tyre' after just a quick look at the ice or gravel notes. So if a tiny patch of ice is *always* there on a particular long straight, it is unlikely to cause any problems and can be disregarded when making up ice notes.

As with making pace notes, the co-driver should log exactly what the driver says about ice and gravel. It follows that someone making ice or gravel notes should talk to the actual drivers on the event so that he knows what they are expecting of him; everything must be geared to aiding the bloke who is going to be at the wheel on the actual rally—notes should not be geared to the vanities of the people making them.

Incidentally, it doesn't really matter how pace notes are marked up with gravel or ice so long as everyone understands the system in use. You could use broken lines to indicate patchy ice or gravel, unbroken lines to show constant ice or snow or whatever. Keep in mind that schedules must allow time for people making ice and gravel notes to mark them up for the actual rally crews. Notes need to have drivers' names and rally numbers on them.

Recceing

The main purpose of a recce is to practise the special stages and make things as easy as possible on the rally itself; the co-driver should therefore plan a recce with care so that no time is wasted. You will need to gather information on garages, hotels, service points, and so on; at key points it might be worth taking Polaroids to give to the mechanics who will actually be at those places on the event. Keep a note of the weather, talk to the locals and try to get an idea of what it's likely to be when you arrive on the rally. During a reconnaissance, try to get an overall feel for the pattern of the rally so that you will be comfortable with it once it starts.

And once it starts, *timekeeping* will be a key part of your job. Have proper equipment and *know how it works*. You don't *have* to have the latest gizmo provided what you do have gives you clearly legible and accurate information about both time and distances.

It is essential that the co-driver understands the regulations for the event as well as the timing system used (not least, what the maximum lateness is before you are excluded).

If crews are to pace themselves properly, they must know how their stage times compare with those of key rivals. A log sheet like this helps the process.

SS	Kankkunen	Biasion	Auriol	Sainz	Alen	Erickson	Wilson	Recalde	Mikkola
1	2.13	2.14	2.13	2.11	2.15	2.15	2.13	2.19	2.16
2	4.41	5.01 Punc	4.42	4.39	4.51	4.47	4.44	5.02	4.46
	6.54	7.15	6.55	6.50	7.06	7.02	6.57	7.21	7.02
3	19.47	19.31	20.40	20.01	21.12	19.54	20.02	21.40	20.11
	26.41	26.46	27.35	26.51	28.18	26.56	26.59	28.01	27.13
4	12.34	12.27	12.42	12.26	12.31	RET	12.39	13.01	12.51
	39.15	39.13	40.17	39.17	40.49	OFF	39.38	41.02	40.04
5	6.11	6.10	RET	6.09	6.14		6.15	6.40	6.20
	45.26	45.23	Susp	45.26	47.03		45.53	47.42	46.24
6	9.40	9.37		9.36	9.42		9.42	10.20	9.47
	55.06	55.00		55.02	56.45		55.35	58.02	56.11
7									
8									
9									
10									
11									
12									

During the event itself, cultivate a sense of time. For example at service points, if you are nervous it's always tempting to say 'We've got five minutes lads' when in fact you've got ten. Be honest, otherwise, as mentioned in the previous chapter, 8-minute jobs won't get done.

Keep a record of your stage times as well as those of the key opposition; use one of the standard forms available. You will find that the serious drivers and co-drivers will give you their correct times. Curiously one or two idiots, for some reason known only to them, lie about their times but you will quickly learn who they are and disregard them.

An awareness of timing will clearly be important when you get to special stage and main *controls* where checking-in is a co-driver's key task.

Keep an eye on food supplies at controls. If you haven't got the luxury of your own mobile catering unit, either try to pinch food from other crews or send a helper for supplies—avoid hot, brightly lit or smoky cafés if possible. At main controls you may need to keep a check on where your driver is. If he's preening himself in front of the TV cameras, don't hesitate to drag him away if you're due to leave; it may make a good story if you do it vigorously enough.

Incidentally, as mentioned earlier if there are bright lights around it's worth wearing dark glasses otherwise your eyes will take time to readjust when you re-start should there be any night driving.

Driving

Co-drivers are unlikely to do a lot of driving, but if they do their aim should be to drive safely so that they give the driver confidence and at the same time care for the car—it is not their role to wear the thing out.

If you have any driving ambitions *suppress* them because the co-driver's seat is not the place to show how quick you are. However, conversely, if you've got any doubts about your driving ability (and too rarely do people have any) it could be worth going to an advanced *road* driving school, rather than a race or rally one, so that you learn sound road techniques.

(Although we stress that the co-driver's seat is not the place to show your driving talents, it is worth recalling that Vic Elford, for many years a co-driver, used vigorously to point out that he was quicker than the drivers he was put with. Everyone smiled politely . . . Vic went on to win the Monte Carlo Rally as a driver.)

During a rally the crew should know and feel exactly what is

Organizers are human and can make mistakes so a key part of a co-driver's job is to double check results.

happening to the car. This is often something that can be discussed on the road sections. If a long repair job needs doing, then thought should be given to whether this can be broken down so that some parts are taken off before a car limps into a halt or control and the second part of the job completed in the next road section. Obviously, this should be discussed with any service crews involved and such discussions may often be over a radio. If so, the co-driver should not only maintain radio discipline himself—using proper call signs, for instance—but he should insist that support crews do too; it's far too easy to prattle away once you've got a microphone in your hand.

Communications should be kept to essential messages and should not divulge information that could be embarrassing or useful to other teams. When approaching a service point a co-driver should make contact with the relevant service crew and give the following information: time the car will arrive at the service point; any work required, in order of importance; time available for the work; and, finally, what tyres and fuel are needed.

When the rally is finally over the co-driver can relax and forget all about it, yes? No! It should be his job to watch for the final results to be posted and he should double-check the stage times. Then, if you are to perform better on the next rally, you must find time for an inquest. What went right? What went wrong? What can be done to correct the latter next time? Were there any organizer's quirks that need to be watched? Were there any problems with particular hotels? Were there good or bad service places? Did the opposition do anything better than you? If so, pinch their ideas.

Keep records of rallies so that you learn by your mistakes because if you do an event in January you will have forgotten it by March, particularly if you do another event in February. In other words: be organized and disciplined. Back to being the business manager . . .

11

Climbing the Ladder

The first thing to remember about building a career in motorsport and climbing the ladder to the top is that *you* must make it happen; no one is likely to do it for you. So maybe you need to go right back to Chapter One and reconsider your motivation. Are you really serious? Serious enough, for instance, to give up your job? Even in the lower branches of racing it may be difficult to hold down 9 to 5 employment *and* do the amount of testing (and sponsorship chasing) needed, while even a mild rally programme may quickly use up your holiday entitlement.

If of course you already have a good sponsor—perhaps through family or business connections—then your task will be a whole lot easier, as it will be if you've got 'it'. Don't ask us to define 'it' too closely, but have you got that certain aura of skill and success around you? You don't need an honours degree as a team manager to tell that a Stewart, Senna, or Sainz has got talent. One of the authors was privileged to be present at an extensive test day at Silverstone when ten drivers tried ten cars, each being given only three laps or so in each car. At least one of the drivers present has since commented that it wasn't really 'fair' (who said motorsport was supposed to be fair?); another—then unknown—driver was quickest in several of the cars and impressed in all of them. Jackie Stewart. Similarly, both authors were privileged to work with Carlos Sainz in his development years and it didn't need much intelligence to see that he'd got 'it'.

Often those who aren't thus blessed complain that it's all a matter of luck. Well, to a small extent of course it is, as it is in any sport—if your horse goes lame before a key showjumping round you can call it bad luck, *provided* the horse has been properly schooled and looked after. Similarly, if a key engineer has an off year just as you join a team, then it may be bad luck. But don't scurry to use luck as an excuse too readily because as the old cliché says (and like all clichés it carries an element of truth), the harder you work, the luckier you will get. If you don't check a groom's credentials before hiring him and he causes a horse to go lame . . . if you don't realize until it's too late that a key designer is mentally exhausted or embroiled in distracting domestic problems . . . is that bad luck or your inefficient approach? The latter we suggest.

Few drivers seem to bother reading anything longer than labels on sauce bottles (even then some just go by the colour), but it really is worth reading about drivers and their careers. In particular, note how two may be equal in a junior category; they may be equal in the next one up but then, as they near the top of the ladder, one will shine while the other will go off the boil. If they have joined different teams the latter may talk about luck, but more often it may be an inability to function as well at a higher level. If it happens to you, try to analyse what is happening. Don't waste time on bitter reflections about what might have been; if you beat a current F1 star in Formula Ford five years ago, so what? You are only as good as your current season.

Of course there will be times when you will have a perfectly valid reason for not winning, but do remember that too many excuses placed end to end become unconvincing and, frankly, are about as interesting as other people's operations.

Set yourself personal objectives because if you don't know where you are going you are unlikely to get there; write your objectives down at the start of a programme then look at them at intervals—if you get wrapped in the minutiae of a championship you may lose sight of where you are hoping to head.

Having set objectives, try to keep up the momentum of your career otherwise it may go cold—sadly, you often see drivers staying too long in a category so that, however quick they are, they get overtaken on the way to stardom by the latest hotshots. And do accept, by the way, that drivers go in and out of fashion, with team managers (often without any logical reason) chasing after the latest wonderman. The fever is as contagious in F1 as in the lower realms of the sport. It's a cruel world.

One of the easiest sports in which to reach the top must be athletics because costs are relatively low and most of it is down to you not your equipment. Unhappily for embryo stars, motorsport is right at the other end of the economic scale and, in addition to the high cost, is hopelessly over-complicated. However, the proliferation of categories and events at least means you should find something that interests you. Above all, if you want to be a top driver then *drive.* In your early career driving almost anything

Above and below *There are countless one-make race series like these for Porsches and Mazdas. Costs can be controlled and competition is likely to be close but don't linger too long in such series if you are ambitious.*

This page and opposite *When racing touring cars you will have the comfort of a roof cover over your head and a large roll cage as well as ample space for sponsors' decals. The choice is almost endless from production saloons for Group N or similar cars, to 'pure' Group A (which has now fallen out of favour) or unique national regulations like those in Germany in which the BMW and Mercedes here are competing. Or you could try NASCAR in America (the photograph shows the Daytona 500) which is much better promoted than most European touring car races.*

is better than sitting at home watching TV.

But what category and car to choose? Should you even design your own car? Agreed, over the years people have managed to combine designing and driving, but with the pace of modern competition you will probably find just one of the two is a full-time job. One advantage of a season spent designing or heavily modifying a car is that it will increase your knowledge of handling and let you work out of your system any pet—but possibly off-beam—theories.

If you plan to go *racing* then one of the formulae restricting the choice of chassis and/or engine is best because the cars should be relatively equal. One-make saloon car races can be competitive, as of course can more highly-tuned saloons, and you do have the advantage of a roof over your head. However, don't stay in saloons overlong because they are not considered really 'serious' and will not be an area where F1 team managers will be scouting for talent. But you once beat an F1 star in an identical saloon? Of *course* you did; history is littered with such examples because the aforesaid F1 driver was either doing it for the money or, more likely, couldn't concentrate because he was laughing at the handling compared with his usual mount.

Sports cars? They can be good little earners and also highly competitive but, again, unlikely to be a career path to F1, at least not while the single-seater ladder keeps throwing up such young talent.

Historic or classic races or rallies won't help your career one jot and don't bother with truck racing either, other than for the driving fees; it is more likely to turn teams off you than on. If you want to progress in racing it is well nigh imperative to stick to the classic single seater route: karts, Formula Ford, Formula Renault, GM, F3, F3000 and then, with luck F1; some of the middle rungs can be jumped.

If you feel you would like to be a *rally* driver then first, and cheapest of all perhaps, is to do one as a co-driver; this will give you experience and a better understanding of both the sport and the co-driver's job. If nothing else it may stop you later in your career from asking your co-driver for another toffee just when he is engrossed in a complicated timing calculation.

Swapping roles can even work between racing and rallying. Race drivers are often too well paid to want to bother, but a few loose special stages can do wonders the next time it rains on the track, while a rally driver may improve his tarmac skills via racing. Carlos Sainz used to race in Formula Fords and Renault 5s and he doesn't get too many complaints about his skills.

As with racing, one-make rally series can be good grounding for

Above *Although numerous manufacturers are now in sports cars (and no category which embraces the world's best known race, Le Mans, can be ignored) the category is unlikely to be as useful a rung on your ladder as single-seater races.*

Below *Race trucks for amusement perhaps but don't expect 'phone calls from any of the F1 team managers if you win.*

Above *'Raid' events like the Paris Daker on which Ari Vatanen is seen here, have their own unique flavour and present special challenges but are unlikely to launch a driver into World Championship rallying.*

Below *Rally crews may learn a lot in one of the one-make championships where, in addition to competing in the overall event, you can also compare your times with people in identical cars. With some series there may be back-up support by way of driving tuition, parts help, and so on.*

Above and below *Formula Ford 1600 and Formula Renault are just two of the many single-seater race categories from which to choose — and you must get into single seaters sooner rather than later if you want to hit the heights.*

rally drivers, especially those that have works support with, say, tyre deals and tuition in preparation and driving techniques (as well as financial support). (By the way, you will remember the advice to get a left-hand drive rally car as soon as possible, won't you?) Although one-make rally championships may be competitive and enjoyable you *must* get onto the 'conventional' Group N then Group A ladder if you hope to get a works drive. Caution: don't assume Group N is safer than A because with some cars you have very similar power but poorer brakes in Group N. All very character building.

In either racing or rallying, you need to consider whether to follow the pack and run a similar car to everyone else or run an oddball. With the latter you will be popular with commentators and you may get noticed; with the former you are likely to get a better parts supply and benchmarks to measure yourself against. In addition, if a driver has loyally campaigned one manufacturer's cars he is less likely to be overlooked in favour of someone with no links with that team.

Whatever the category, if your car is uncompetitive then clearly you are not going to shine. So do remember the points we considered in the chapter on finding a car. Does the factory help its runners with technical information and parts? Don't blame them if the latest parts are not on sale immediately—in racing they may want to keep a competitive edge a little longer, while in rallying they may want to confirm that a part is reliable before producing it in quantity.

Is a car known to be a bit of a sod to drive? Do you really need that extra challenge? If, incidentally, you don't find out that your car is uncompetitive until the season has started—as sometimes happens in, say, F3—weigh up all the information you have (getting expert advice if you need it) and then be *decisive.* If you are going to swap horses (always supposing you can afford to) then do it and get the new horse galloping as quickly as you can.

Apart from the car, what about the category you are planning to do—is it 'hot'? If it has previously thrown up stars, then team managers may be watching it for new ones. Does the series get good media coverage?

Moving from horses to fish for an analogy—what is the size of the pond? If your funding or experience is limited it may be better to win a *regional* race or rally championship than limp in fifth in a national one because it can be made to look better on a CV; class wins are quite useful here, too, as are awards of any sort that matter. Are you from, say, East Anglia? Are you the only one from there doing a particular championship? Then get someone (your father if necessary) to present an award for the 'Best East Anglian

One sure-fire way of climbing to the top is to impress everyone with an unexpected performance on a major event. Francois Delecour did this by leading the 1991 Monte Carlo Rally until near the end, clearly signalling to the rally world that a new superstar had arrived.

Driver'. The line in your CV or sponsor-seeking brochure will be cheap at the price.

It is quite easy to suffer from self-delusion or, worse, start believing your own press clippings. Be wary of this trap if you become a big fish in what you think is a significant pond but is in fact relatively shallow. Some years the British Open Rally Championship falls into this category—it gets reasonable media coverage and is 'Britain's Best', yet there are only a handful of serious cars and no foreign stars. It could be better in such cases to tackle a national championship in another country because facing tougher competition over different terrain is likely to carry you ahead of your domestic opponents. Apart from the experience, you should be able to generate useful media coverage if you are operating in foreign parts, and people won't be able to vet your tall stories. However, before you get too taken with the suggestion, do check that you would be eligible for the events—some championships are restricted to nationals.

We mentioned earlier the importance of driving, driving, and driving to get experience. Rallymen may even stray into autotests to fill in their time; race drivers may decide to drive in more than one category (if nothing else this may help to learn new circuits). Caution though: don't *over* stretch your resources, energy, or time. Commuting backwards and forwards between two race meetings by helicopter sounds desperately dramatic and will get a media mention—but your results (and does much else matter?) may be better if you concentrate properly on one series.

In many categories of motorsport you will have a lot of fun, make plenty of friends, and thoroughly enjoy the scene. That's all very well BUT if you plan to reach the top, sooner rather than later you will have to stop playing happy campers and move on up that ladder. You *must* be stretched.

How long should you stay in one category? One answer is: until you've stopped learning. So the quicker you learn, the faster you will climb the ladder. Learning means being more than just a gorilla driver (another banana?) who simply steers and presses pedals; you must do more than that and, for example, learn to 'read' an event; evaluate your competition; judge when or if to change tyres . . . plus the myriad of other things needed to become a *complete* race or rally driver. Even learn how to become at one with your car—sit in it quietly, touch the switches, get the feel of the pedals, note where the gauges are. Ignore any scoffers who disrupt your meditations; just make them the first you spray with your winner's champagne, because if you do absorb the car so that you become a part of it, then you will drive better and be more likely to win.

Traditionally, drivers spend at least one full season in a category, but if you choose badly and find, for instance, that you are totally dominating your scene and sense you've learnt all you can, then move on up quicker if you can afford it—better to spend the second half of a season becoming attuned to the next higher category ready for a full attack on it the following year. However, there is another aspect to consider (as there so often is in this great sport of ours) and that is that if you climb too fast you may find yourself barred from dropping back down a step on the ladder because of the regulations. Even if you are allowed to step down, you may find yourself in a 'no win' situation as far as your reputation is concerned—if you win you hear 'Well, of course he should', if you don't 'He's passed it and it was all a flash in the pan'. Your call.

If you find your season is not going well and you've no hope of winning a championship, or are running out of money, then cut out either the far-flung events or the least important ones in media terms or, most sensible of all, the events you are least likely to do well in.

As only one car wins a race it follows that the majority of drivers are not in winning vehicles; many are not even in potentially winning ones. If, for whatever reason, you have to endure several seasons in poor machinery do accept that it will be very difficult to re-establish yourself as a quick talent. The fact that you have been held back by your cars may, sadly, even mean that the edge has gone from your skill and/or motivation but . . . they do come back, so don't despair. Just recognize the severity of the task.

People also come back after a spate of crashes. In fact some people hold the view that if 100 is perfect driving and driver A varies between 95 and 105 then, while he is likely to be off the road or track from time to time, after exploring the frontiers through the sound barrier he may well become a 100 driver. On the other hand if driver B starts at 85 and decides to slowly work his way up to 100, he may stick at around 97. Mr B may become a good reliable driver but A will set the pulses racing and end up with the flat in Monte Carlo. Important note: we are NOT encouraging you to have crashes, we are simply describing what seems to happen.

Setting pulses racing is a good way of climbing the ladder, which is why winning one in three events is probably better than finishing third on all three, and there may be other ways of exciting people than slogging through a championship—the Formula Ford Festival at Brands Hatch has long been 'one to win' and, coming at the end of the year, a good time to be attracting attention and a drive for the following year. A rally driver could try staking all on trying to shine on the first day of the RAC Rally or go off to one or two events abroad. Unhappily, we can't include a neat decision tree to help you up the ladder because even though the F1 stars are now coming up through fairly clear single-seater paths, a maverick can still make it and get a team's attention.

As a part way staging post to a full works drive, can you be 'semi-works', running as the factory B team or whatever? Some manufacturers have a policy of nurturing talent through from a very early stage, although the jury is still out as to whether this is a Good Thing for either party: a driver may not wish to be linked to a manufacturer at certain stages in his career, while however much a manufacturer invests in a driver they are likely to find someone will blow in his ear and offer him more money if he shows real star quality.

Perhaps you could liaise with the factory and do events which they aren't contesting? If they are attacking a world or national championship, why not seek support in tackling a European or regional programme to complement rather than fight their official plan? Be prepared for mixed emotions if you come head-to-head with a works team and beat them in the same type of car; realistic team managers should sit up and notice you (the press certainly will) but the less bright and more parochial ones may be a bit piqued.

As a bold alternative, if you know or suspect that a new manufacturer is to enter the arena in a year or so, then campaigning their products now may help you because they may feel a certain obligation to you when they come on stream.

Despite its delusions of grandeur, motorsport is quite a small, insular world and you will fairly rapidly get to know, or know about, the decision makers. How you approach or lobby them, whether by 'phone, letter, or direct, is up to you. We deal with self-promotion later but *don't* assume team managers have supernatural powers when it comes to driver selection. F1 team chiefs have little time to go talent spotting, and it is virtually impossible to test rally drivers, which is why manufacturers are likely to tell you 'we only pick rally drivers with considerable success, either with their own cars or with other works teams'. The stakes are too high for them to do much else.

If your approaches get you a test drive then try to avoid bending the car, but do try to impress. It may not be sensible, but first impressions do count and if you do ten highly competent runs and another driver is more erratic *but* does a couple of dramatically quick times, he may be the one to be remembered. The other approach may perhaps lead to a job as a test driver (someone to grind through the kilometres sorting suspensions, testing engines, and so on), but be careful here that you don't simply become seen as a useful but over-familiar part of the furniture. Incidentally, if you are test driving for a team be sure to establish the objectives for the day—suspension sorting, durability running, or whatever.

The only guaranteed way to climb is to get results. Let's dream for a while and assume you've done so well that teams are fighting over you. (Curious how that conjures up a vision of sharks . . .) Things to consider before gracing a team with your signature include:

- Is the team on an 'up' or a 'down'?
- If it's on an 'up', are the key people staying for the next season. If it's on a 'down', do you really believe any promised changes will make all the difference?
- Does it seem fully committed or are the people just playing at motorsport? A lot are.
- Has the team got adequate resources, not least money?
- Has the team operated in the category before? If not, will they be able to handle it?
- Do you feel compatible with them? Will you be able to work with them? It's a people business and, just like selecting an advertising or PR agency, if you don't feel

comfortable with them the chemistry may not work.

- How compatible will you be with any other drivers in the team?

Don't misunderstand the last couple of points. We are *not* suggesting that to be successful everything needs to be sweetness and light. Conflict can set the adrenalin flowing and disagreements in a team, honestly discussed, can lead to greater synergy than if everyone is demurely nodding agreement all the time. But after the discussions everyone must agree on one course of action and *back it.*

Morose loners do make the top because, after all, race and rally driving are different to team sports like soccer and egos are only to be expected; but nevertheless, as a team driver (and therefore a focal point) you can actually lift a team by improving the spirit within it; too often drivers appear under the impression that they are doing a team a favour by deigning to drive for it. And if you doubt the uplifting value of teamwork consider how, in every soccer World Cup, teams from places you've never even heard of play out of their skins ... because of team spirit.

To help the team-building process:

1. Establish from the start what the team expects from you. Do they want you there all the time helping, or would they prefer you to just turn up at events?
2. Let the team get used to you. Don't charge in throwing your weight around.
3. Work hard to build a relationship with the key engineer. Learn to give him intelligent feedback. Be computer literate but learn sensibly to balance data with experience.
4. Remember if you are a neurotic nit-picking driver wanting things changed all the time then, ye gods, you'd better deliver the results.
5. At least stay on speaking terms with the other driver(s) in the team. There will obviously be rivalry on events and if this is healthy then it will lift the whole standard; but if it leads to in-fighting and bickering within the team then it will be very *un*healthy. While advocating that you remain on reasonable terms with the other driver(s), we would also stress that you try very hard to out-perform them in the early events in the season so that you establish a psychological supremacy and, to some extent, become the number one driver, getting the best treatment. You don't have to put on a white coat and become the team psychologist but the basics of team-building aren't difficult to jot down, though they may be less easy to implement. For example, there must be clear objectives. These

should be realistic but with an element of stretch.

Although team managers tend to be strong characters they should still be encouraged to push authority down. Everyone should be *involved*. As an example, if someone makes the tea, let *them* choose the make and buy it.

A more direct way of encouraging team members to feel involved will be to share a percentage of winnings as a bonus—the system used is unimportant *provided* it is understood by everyone and is deemed to be fair. While we're talking of teams, don't forget that team awards on events often get very few entries; link with other drivers to try to win them because there can be press mentions or pictures as a result.

And finally, all other things being equal, a team will work better if there is just a touch of humour. For this reason if you join a foreign team, try to learn their language—they will appreciate your efforts and you will provide a constant source of merriment for them.

But—and it is a fairly substantial 'but'—however well you manoeuvre into a team, and however well you clamber up the ladder, it won't all go well. If you hit problems then the way in which you cope with them will be a good measure of whether you are likely to really make it. If you lose events, then while you will, or should, burn to do better next time, do be a realistic loser: analyse why you lost. Was it you or the car? If the latter, was it through bad planning, poor preparation, lack of testing, or what? What corrective action is needed? Similarly, if you keep having accidents, try to analyse why and, if you can't find corrective action, consider giving up.

If, unhappily, you are injured, well, the sport appears to expect its heroes to do dramatic things and drive strapped up or whatever; Eric Carlsson perhaps set the fashion all those years ago when he won an RAC Rally wrapped in bandages from Boots simply because he had to wait too long in a local hospital to get what proved to be broken ribs treated. Caution in such heroics: take specialist medical advice and, if coming back too soon seems likely to prolong your full recovery time, wait for the next race or rally. Console yourself with the thought that although it is nice if your climb up the ladder is straightforward, drivers *have* got a second wind and made dramatic comebacks after their careers had apparently slumped.

If you finally reach the top, enjoy it because it's quite a hard sport and you are only as good as your last event. To try to stay ahead, analyse your success; did you still make mistakes which, if corrected, would make you even better? And with success do try

Above and below *Motorsport has to be taken seriously if you want to win: John Taylor and Carlos Sainz discuss tactics on a Spanish championship rally — but it needn't always be serious: the amusement of Malcolm Wilson and Stuart Turner was caused when they each suggested the driving fee they had in mind for the following season.*

to keep the same sized helmet won't you? Then all you've got to decide is when to stop. When it becomes dangerous; when it becomes just a job; when you start embarrassing yourself. Otherwise if you are still competent and enjoying it, why not soldier on? Only one point to keep in mind: if you build a famous name and hope to trade on it after you have stopped racing, *don't* go on after your peak otherwise you may devalue your reputation, with the public remembering your twilight years instead of the glorious ones.

Footnote for co-drivers

If you want to reach the top as a co-driver, first learn the basics on club events and then get into rallies using pace notes as soon as possible (preferably events in Europe).

Whilst it is nice to form a cosy partnership with a driver, if yours is clearly not going anywhere or, worse, scares you to death, then be ruthless and find someone else.

If you get your chance with a works team bear in mind that they will want TOTAL reliability above all else. Offer to help in the admin of the team and make constructive suggestions, which is why you should keep records of such things as hotels, service points, and so forth on the rallies you do.

12

Personal Affairs

This chapter considers how you should handle yourself away from the competition scene—not an unimportant side of a driver's life because if you can't manage your personal affairs properly you are unlikely to be able to cope with a climb to the top. We know you are fed up with reading the word but: plan. The more you plan ahead and get yourself organized, the better you will be able to handle the unexpected last minute problems that are inevitable in the sport. Consider how often F1 teams run extensive winter test programmes . . . and then have to work all-nighters just before the first race. Why should you be any different?

You will have contact with a lot of people during a motorsport career (fellow drivers, organizing clubs, the media, team members, *et al.*), and part of your self-management should be to aim to be reliable in your dealings with them. Quite apart from the fact that life will probably be more pleasant, the motorsport grapevine is an active one and while you don't have to be over-smooth and obsequious, word will quickly spread if you are unreliable or offensive. As an aside, young drivers would perhaps be surprised at how often team managers, who are deadly rivals on events, compare notes about events *and drivers.* So if you cheat either on events or in your personal behaviour, it's likely to rebound. And incidentally, however poor the driving of a fellow competitor who causes you to go off, *don't* then set about him with your feet or fists; use words to express your opinions instead. If you resort to violence you deserve banning for life (not just having your wrist mildly slapped as sometimes happens) because if you can't control your emotions, then you are not safe when competing.

Dress

Your planning and attention to detail should extend to the way you dress. Before the dead hand of sponsorship neutered so much sport, race and rally drivers were expected to be slightly larger than life characters and to some extent this still applies; but don't be so bizarre in your behaviour or dress that you frighten the horses, or, worse, the sponsors. Bear in mind that if you are in a business meeting and you are the only one scruffily dressed among the suits, then you will appear a bit odd and may be at a disadvantage when negotiating. You may also be at a disadvantage if you appear to be a total ignoramus so, for instance, it is worth at least glancing through one of the more serious daily newspapers so that you are loosely aware of what is happening in the big wide world; if a world-shattering event is happening and you are blissfully unaware of it you may not be seen by potential sponsors as committed and single-minded, but as crass and stupid.

Even if your budget won't stretch to colour-keyed clothing it *should* stretch to soap, so while you may appear unkempt, you shouldn't appear unwashed. And dirty finger nails on a boardroom table won't endear you to sponsors either.

Motorsport is considered (or alleged) to be an up-to-the-minute activity so your dress and hairstyle should at least be in fashion, even though the authors do feel that their plus-fours and spats display a certain flair.

Following fashion shouldn't extend to the latest lager craze. Get used to champagne by all means . . . but as something to be sprayed when you win, not drunk. If a glass or two of wine the evening before an event helps you relax and sleep better, then be our guest; but if you become a more boozy character and spend your time propping up the bar, don't be surprised if your car breaks because your mechanics have followed your example and are propping up the other end. We hope we're not sounding too censorious (although we suspect that we are), but we are trying to emphasize that to get to the top in motorsport you will need to have everything going for you; until there is any evidence that smoking and drinking makes you a better driver, why bother?

Fitness

And here comes some further finger wagging. We mentioned it way back in the book but . . . you will watch your weight and keep fit, won't you? Driving can be hard physically as well as mentally; the fitter you are the quicker you are likely to be. Should you have a coach? No, not something on wheels to transport your growing army of fans, but a person to guide you on your approach to your job. Well, if top athletes, tennis players and so on, perform better with someone to guide them, why not you? Take care, though, to find someone with whom you are compatible—which means going back to the self-analysis to help you decide if you need a dominant coach, who will push and bully you into doing things, or more of a friend and confidant. If you think a coach's 'theories' are way-out and impractical, then you aren't going to feel comfortable with them; in fact, if you get too off-beam you could make your performance worse. But someone to help you with a diet and fitness routine may make a positive contribution, as may an older driver to turn to for advice or act as a shoulder to moan on. But just remember: when the flag drops . . . it's down to you, so don't lean on people so much for psychological support that you feel lost because they aren't actually sitting in the car with you.

Developing a ritualistic approach to your craft may help you perform better. You don't have to stick pins in effigies of FIA dignitaries—not that we're against it, mind—but just as a sport star always puts on his left shoe first, or always opens the door with his left hand before a race, so might you find a pattern of behaviour soothing. Don't laugh—if you think about it you will probably recognize that you have already formed a ritual without realizing it. *What* you do doesn't matter, the concentration which it helps to harness does. You may even find sex before an event assists you to harness your resources, although it is discourteous to keep other competitors waiting.

Road driving

Consider adopting a programmed approach to *road* driving too. We are not advocating a check-capped and stringback gloved approach, but a disciplined 'cockpit check' similar to the one you would use in your competition car will help make it become automatic. And *learn* from your road driving: be aware and assess things—if there are two cars parked in the distance, test yourself on which one is nearest as you approach; if you are a rally driver consider how you would grade the corners if you were making pace notes. If a car pulls out with dust all over it, note if it then pulls across into the cement works further along. See the point—cultivate an *awareness* of what is happening. It will all be happening a lot faster on a track or special stage but the sharper your reflexes and the more aware you are, the better you will cope.

Two final points on road driving:
1. Are you actually any good at it? It doesn't follow that you will be, but you'll look a bit silly if, as a superstar, you can't even reverse properly.
2. If you *can* drive well on the road don't assume others have got your skills. Make allowances.

Administration

That was road manners. Next: business manners. We believe you should handle your own admin, at least in your early days, so that you become familiar with entry forms and the like. As the workload rises you will find companies specializing in handling entries for you and, further up the tree, you may decide to appoint a full blown 'agent' to act on your behalf, negotiating contracts, and maybe handling all your business affairs. Two notes of caution: some drivers' careers have been blighted by over-greedy agents asking for far more than their clients were worth, while an increasing number of team managers seem reluctant to deal via a third party; perhaps they feel that if a driver needs wet-nursing to negotiate a contract, he'll be too precious to make a positive contribution to a team. But if you feel you need that third party and are prepared to pay the commission, which may be up to one third of your earnings, then be sure everything is put in writing to avoid court cases later.

Whatever arrangement you have, you will need a room or at least a specific area to use as an office. This may be in the place where your car is prepared or it may be a spare bedroom in your home (the use of which can be charged against tax). Wherever it is, you will need certain essentials, of which the first is of course a *diary*. Log the dates of races and test days, make them sacrosanct, and as far as possible keep the time around them free. You will probably find the latest time-management system irresistible but the actual sytem is immaterial provided that you know where you are scheduled to be at given times.

Correspondence

Similarly, it's not important what system you have to handle your other admin provided you can understand it, although the simpler it is, the less time it will take. Get into the habit of answering correspondence quickly; problems don't get any easier through procrastination. Keep copies of key letters and bear in mind that the design and quality of your stationery says something about you, so give a little thought to it; most of the franchised quick print shops offer a design service as well as 'starter packs' of business cards, letterheads, and so on.

You will probably find a cheap second-hand office filing cabinet perfectly adequate to store all your documentation; one drawer at least should be dedicated to accounts.

Finance

If you are an innocent about business affairs then a bright, user-friendly accountant may be even more comfort to you than a fitness coach or Swedish masseuse. As we have stressed, you need to budget carefully, you need cash flow forecasts, a bank account, credit card(s), etc, etc.

You and/or your accountant must let your bank manager know what you are up to, and do remember that bank managers, like sponsors and team managers, don't like surprises, at least not unhappy ones. If things are going wrong on the financial front, speak up early, don't rely on wishful thinking to make it all better. For the same reason don't build into budgets too much reliance on bonus payments for successes—use these, if any, for extras not essentials. And don't put too much in the plus column for appearance fees either—the supermarkets won't be clammering for you to cut the opening tapes for quite a while yet. You've read that American sports stars have started charging for autographs? Stop dreaming.

Being in touch

As you accumulate essential equipment, keep in mind that you need to be in touch and contactable so let key people know your address and 'phone number. And talking of 'phones, you may decide to turn your car or service vehicle into a mobile office with a computer and fax machine for your in-car 'phone, plus whatever technology arrives next for data transfer.

Having installed the latest communication equipment, don't then waste it by clearing off for, say, a long skiing holiday just when contracts are being organized for the following season. And even if you *have* got your drive fixed, are you sure skiing makes sense? We don't want to wrap you in cotton wool, but will you be able to get into your car with a leg in plaster? If you can, don't forget to place sponsors' stickers on the cast.

Travel

Even if you don't go skiing, you will probably travel abroad at some point to further your race or rally career. Try to use one of the travel agents specializing in the sport (one may even handle your particular category) because the last minute problems that occur in motorsport may panic a more conventional agent. Not least, of course, you will need slick handling of cars, parts, customs clearance, and so on. Incidentally, as air travel gets busier and delays through baggage searches get longer, try to operate with hand baggage only—you may save hours.

Health

To further your career you may race or rally in obscure far-flung places (you may well get financial inducements to do so), but if so you will need even more care. Look into the health requirements and consult your doctor well before you go to see if any jabs are needed. If you require special medicines remember you may need supporting documentation to take them into some countries to avoid charges of drug running; be sure your team knows of your needs too and whether you are allergic to certain treatments. Don't use drugs purely in an attempt to enhance your driving by the way.

Establish the position over the cost of medical treatment abroad—whether there is a reciprocal agreement with your own country or if you need to arrange special insurance. Have a regular dental check; toothache is no fun anywhere, least of all if you are not sure of local dentistry standards.

When you arrive in far-flung places, take all the sensible precautions over food and drink, and watch the sun, too—you won't have quite your usual delicate touch on the pedals if the tops of your feet are blistering with sunburn.

Jet lag? Well if you ever graduate to driving in other continents beware of jetting in just before an event. Some experts even reckon it takes one day to get over one hour of time change. You probably won't be able to allow that long but help yourself by, for instance, moving around on planes to restore circulation and watching your intake of food and drink. Drivers seem to react to jet lag in different ways so experiment and, if you find a routine that seems to work for you (whether staying on your domestic time clock or whatever) then stick to it.

Legal

Coming down to earth and to end on a more sombre note, have you got a legal adviser? And, for instance, have you made a will? Unless your only asset is a signed copy, slightly foxed, of Eion Young's latest book catalogue, you really ought to make a will. You may become rich and famous faster than you think and in the giddy excitement you may forget to take the simple legal step. If you then die and don't leave a will your assets will be distributed according to the statutory regulations, with which you may not agree—a live-in partner wouldn't benefit, for instance, unless you were actually married.

The same legal adviser may help with contracts. Obviously, you should avoid chaining yourself to a team or sponsor for eternity but, equally, you should try not to take endless weeks in considering a contract. The authors know of several instances where a season has ended (quite happily) before the actual contracts between drivers, teams and sponsors had finally been exchanged.

Unhappily, you may need legal advice if protests end up in the courts. We say 'unhappily' because events should really be won at the wheel—try not to become a barrack room lawyer. We believe *every* race or rally should be decided there and then just as most other sports are—penalty shoot-outs in soccer aren't totally satisfactory, but at least everyone goes home knowing who has won. Drivers and entrants who get wrapped in procedural or technical arguments lose sight of a simple fact, that motorsport is, or should be, appealing to a wide audience and a 'win' that is not announced until after months of legal wrangles is valueless. Worse, the whole procedure makes the sport look silly.

Your accountant and/or legal adviser will be able to advise you about *insurance* (they may of course have a vested interest, via commission, in selling you some) and there are also companies specializing in cover for motorsport. As well as covering your car for competition, for which you may be advised to use one of the brokers specializing in motorsport (you may need medical treatment when you learn the cost), you should also be protected yourself. The degree of insurance you require may depend on whether you are married or single, whether you have an outstanding mortgage, and so on. 'It won't happen to me?' We hope it won't, but it happens to somebody fairly often so you should be covered, even to the extent of receiving an income for the rest of your life if you are disabled. Obviously you should check that any insurance you have does not specifically exclude motorsport.

Other points in this rather sombre area:

- Is your insurance valid in private planes? It should be.
- Do any dependants—your wife, for instance—know about your affairs, where documents are kept and so on? It's even worth drawing up a list of 'what to do if the worst happens'.

If, as we hope, you have a long and successful motorsport career, consider funnelling some of your hopefully high earnings into a pension plan. You may even consider funnelling them into overseas bank accounts. Back to your advisers—if you dream up a complicated scheme and think you are avoiding tax, bear in mind that the taxman may think you are *evading* it; his silence may simply mean he is letting you ripen ready for plucking. Get good advice, as you should if you decide to live abroad.

A final thought on personal affairs. From time to time give some thought to what you will do when you stop driving and, maybe, put preliminary plans in hand now, while your name is hot, rather than later.

You don't need such advice because you are going to be World Champion and will never need to work again? Well, that's all right then. But you'll probably get there quicker if you are well funded, and being well-known may help you to attract that all-important sponsorship, so let us move on to consider how to promote yourself.

13

Self-promotion

Modest person that you are, you may find the theme of this chapter abhorrent, but think about the motorsport pyramid for a moment. At the top there is usually only one or maybe two truly outstanding F1 stars at any time; in fact in some years—although there will of course always be a World Champion—there may be no driver great enough to place alongside the Fangios, Stewarts, Prosts, and Co. Similarly in rallying, there are very few genuine stars during any one era. Assuming that there are 10,000 drivers out there hoping to reach the top (your guess at the number is as good as ours; whatever it is, it's a lot), that means the odds are 10,000 to 1 against you being the best. Even if 10,000 is too high an estimate, the odds are still pretty grim against you reaching the top of that pyramid (or mountain if you prefer—in fact the lack of oxygen at high altitudes perhaps explains some of the bizarre behaviour that sometimes occurs in F1).

What this means is that as the motorsport pyramid broadens towards its base, there are more and more drivers on an equal level, and as well as sheer talent they will need everything else going for them too—and that includes promoting themselves away from the track or special stage.

You are convinced that you are that one in 10,000? Congratulations. Just mind your head doesn't jam in the doorway as you leave. If you are not, then spare the time to read this chapter, bearing in mind that you don't *have* to self-promote or learn to cope with the media. It will just make things easier if you do, because whether you like the idea or not, you are in show business and if other competitors are clammering for attention and you are silent, you may get bypassed; the better known you become the better chance you will have of getting sponsorship and drives and, perhaps not least important, even time off work in your early years because you become something of a local celebrity. (Sensible employers may of course ponder whether you've really got your mind on your job if you are busy chasing stardom in motorsport, but that's another matter.)

We hope we've convinced you that public relations, marketing—call it what you will—can help a driver's career. It can also help promote the sport itself, and in this context do try to be *upbeat*; too often drivers reaching the top moan and generally act as if they've had haemorrhoid transplants, which doesn't do a lot for the activity which gave them their lavish lifestyle. Be more positive.

Agents

If the idea of hustling on your own behalf is too much, then either consider doing it under another name (forming a token company for the purpose) or use an agent to handle PR for you. If you note fellow competitors getting coverage, then ask them how they do it (you may have to ask drivers in other categories because your direct rivals may not wish to tell you). Keep an eye on enthusiast, marketing, and sponsorship magazines because they often carry ads for agents.

Remember you don't need any formal qualifications to act as a PR or marketing agent and there is quite a lot of hype around, so it is up to you to check people out carefully. Follow up references, talk to agents' other clients, and, above all, ask to meet the people who would be working on your account. Do you feel you would get on with them? If not, find someone else.

Having selected an agent, thrash out carefully what each side is expecting of the other, determine payment terms, and then put things in writing. Set objectives—such as so many photographs in so many papers, or whatever—otherwise how will you know if the link has worked? But *don't* expect miracles. With the growth of sponsorship almost every sport is fighting for media attention and national newspapers are unlikely to stop a print run to cover the news that you've just finished third in your class.

Basic planning

Once you have decided how you are going to handle PR, spare time to consider (with an agent if you have one) what 'part' you are going to play. In showbusiness there may only be room for one great character comedian or one top impressionist at a time. Similarly, in motorsport if there is already a Flying Doctor, Flying

Finn, Matador, Bonking Butcher, or whatever, then that slot has been pre-empted and you need to consider how else you can position yourself. Don't get us wrong—we are not suggesting you should take acting lessons and it won't work if you try to behave too far out of character; but you *should* consider what you want to be—the good guy or the bad, the ice cool or emotional driver, or whatever. The media do like to hang convenient labels on people; make it easy in your case. And by the way, what is your name? No, this is not a trick question to test your IQ but to point out that if you are called, say, Napoleon Stringbirtle it may not trip off peoples' tongues quite like Jackie Stewart or Nigel Mansell. Either change your name, or try to get known as 'AJ' or whatever.

Bear in mind that you don't have to strut or be strident to get attention; all things being equal, the public aren't overfond of big heads. In fact you should make a conscious effort to get on with people; *of course* you need to be single-minded and popularity won't win races, but it may stop rivals deliberately trying to block you and it will impress sponsors if you clearly have a rapport with spectators. Similarly, make an effort to go to prizegivings and post-event parties—the club official you meet today may be the steward you appear in front of tomorrow. And resist the temptation to be facetious when filling in commentators' information sheets—they are the guys' working tools, treat them sensibly, and you will probably get better attention from the commentators.

Having established how you want to position yourself, you need some basic PR tools: a neatly set-out fact sheet about yourself, appropriate photographs of you and your car, regular press releases plus, possibly, video clips of the ensemble in action; sponsors may well provide some of this material for you (as well as stickers for kids), but until you've found a sponsor you'll have to do it yourself. The fact sheet doesn't need to be on expensive parchment but any information you send out will be fighting a lot of other bumf for attention so it makes sense to have striking A4 press release paper—maybe with 'NEWS FROM ABC MOTORSPORT', or whatever, at the top.

Mailing lists

Having information about yourself is no use unless you have somewhere to send it and a key tool will be an address list, which should include 'phone and fax numbers. Local libraries will have reference books of newspaper and magazine addresses and, as it's a volatile world, keep an eye open at your newsagents for new publications—they may be fertile ground for your news, but get in

quick in case they fold after a few issues.
Your address list should include:

- Key motoring journalists on the enthusiast magazines, as well as those on national newspapers that regularly give space to motorsport. Get to know them if possible because team managers do read their pieces and often discuss drivers with them.
- Local, regional, and national newspapers. Don't neglect free newspapers.
- Local radio and TV stations.
- Local and regional business magazines.
- 'Stringers', ie local journalists who feed stories to the nationals.

Plus—well, plus whoever you can think of: local factory newsletters, church and school magazines, hobby magazines, and so on. You probably won't send every press release to all the publications on your list but you should plan, for example, to send your old school magazine one feature a year. And talking of features, if magazines run 'a day in the life of' or 'my favourite pet' pages, could one be written about you? Keep looking for opportunities, then follow them up. Could you get mileage out of a genuine project with a local charity, for example?

If you are entering an event or championship (including those abroad) contact the press office and/or the sponsors to see if there are mutual promotional opportunities.

Develop a 'PR Checklist' of things to do before and after each event as well as on a regular basis out of season—communicate with sponsors, send press releases to local papers, 'phone local radios, and so on. Add to the checklist as you learn. You may care to jot comments about journalists on your address list, but care: use a code and put DOP instead of 'doddery old prat' in case he ever sees it.

'Launder' your mailing list at regular intervals; it looks, and is, inefficient to send three or four press releases to the same person, especially if he left the paper some years ago, yet people do it. Motorsport people also persist in sending out Christmas cards with pictures of themselves in competition cars on them. Rarely seasonal and frequently tacky, although it probably won't stop you doing the same.

Press releases

You've got your neatly printed press release paper and a list of important people. All you need now is some news to send out. The key people—team members, relations, sponsors, etc—may need an information bulletin spelling out what the event is, where and what time it starts, plus details of the press office and where you and the team are staying. If you build up good links with key journalists they may appreciate being on the list for this bulletin too.

As far as press releases to a wider audience are concerned, remember you are not writing a Great Novel but imparting information, so a release needs to tell people *who* is involved in *what*, *where* it takes place, and *when*, and maybe *why* (e.g. 'it's the third round in a 10-event championship').

Type press releases on one side of A4 paper with double spacing and wide margins so that recipients have room to add or modify.

Team members must be properly informed about arrangements for events and, as here, instructions can sometimes run to several pages.

TEAM INFORMATION		CONFIDENTIAL
SECTION		PAGE
1	TIMETABLE AND ROUTE SUMMARY	1
2	RECONNAISSANCE	2
3	ENTRIES	4
4	TRAVEL TO START	5
5	HOTEL RESERVATIONS	6
6	SERVICE PERSONNEL AND VEHICLES	10
7	SERVICE INFORMATION	12
8	TYRES AND WHEELS	14
9	SCRUTINEERING, START, ETC.	15
10	PRESS AND PUBLIC RELATIONS	16
11	DEALERS	16
12	RALLY HEADQUARTERS	17
13	RETURN TRAVEL FROM FINISH	18
14	CLOTHING	19
15	PERSONNEL LIST	20
16	ROUTE SYNOPSIS	21
17	MAPS: ROUTE OUTLINE	
	TOWN PLANS	
	PRESS DAY LAYOUT	
	SCRUTINEERING	
18	EMERGENCY PHONES	

Ideally, any press release you send out should be on specially headed paper because it will be fighting for space with countless others.

Put the most important news first, because if journalists want to shorten a relase they will crop the last paragraph first. Include a *quote* to add life to your news and ensure the release has the name and 'phone number of someone journalists can contact if they need more information.

Other points about press releases:

- Under- rather than overstate your targets. If you say you aim to get in the first six and finish third, it will look like a success; if you announce in advance you are going to win then finish third you will be deemed to have failed.

- If you have a long tale to tell, then mail a one-page summary with a more detailed attachment.

If you have good links with a magazine or particular journalist then writing a letter to them may be as effective as a press release. This is the result of such an approach to Autosport, *which, incidentally, you should regard as essential reading.*

ARRIVE 'N DRIVE

EAST LONDON RACING ORGANIZATION

Jeff Williams, 70 Uplands Road, Woodford Bridge, Essex, IG8 8JW, England.

Tel: 081-505 0750

FORMULA FIRST AND FORD RACEHIRE AND GENERAL RACECAR PREPARATION

Dear Marcus,

&nclosed are a few details regarding my new Arrive 'n Drive scheme. It's the same East London Racing Organ-ization (Racehire), but we are trying to establish it as the Team to start your racing career off with, when you have competed

The reason for the name change is to try an establish what we do in the title. "First Time Racing" for instance is great because it tells you exactly what they are, for beginners. You would be surprised at the amount of calls I get from race school pupils who do not know anything about the next step on the racing ladder.

We have al

.located by unequal length ones.
.he 1781cc Volkswagen Golf GTI

.o the
.ston, Jamaica,
chassis were shaken down,
ton Park. Some 20 examples
apparently been sold.

Racenire, unfortunatly
we are not as cheap as
best deal for descent
our leaflets that sh
hopefully get movin
overheads, our test
Ford £II50.

can use. If you re
contact.

Simply arrive 'n' drive...

Jeff Williams has renamed his East London Racing Organisation racehire business Arrive 'n' Drive.

Williams, perhaps *the* expert in low cost, big value, racehire deals (having contested 190 races himself, on minimal budgets), continues to provide competitive, well-presented cars for both Formula First and FF1600.

Often dubbed 'the Ken Tyrrell of Formula First', Jeff has helped such drivers as Simon Packford ("the

best"), Andy Gregory and Marcus Simmons to get started, only to see them move on to more opulent outfits.

He is now trying to raise the profile of his Essex-based team, making it more even attractive to racing school and karting graduates.

Costs for test day and race programmes (including entry fees and car insurance) currently start at £1050 (First) and £1100 (FF1600). All you do is Arrive 'n' Drive...

DRIVER TO WATCH: JASON PLATO

and look for some sponsorship. I was getting really fed up, I knew I was good enough."

- Put a date on your release.
- Consider when to fax or post releases. Establish when publications close for press and try to be well ahead of these times.
- Don't attempt to 'embargo' news—that is, put on a release that it should be held until a certain date. You may very occasionally need to do this to comply with a sponsor's wishes but otherwise your news is unlikely to be deemed important enough by journalists for it to be carrying an embargo, so they won't obey it even if they bother to print your story at all.
- Don't forget *seasonal* stories. You can safely assume that Christmas, New Year, and Easter will keep rolling round at the same time each year: can you think of a topical story that will appeal to journalists?
- Don't be afraid to recycle old ideas. If they got coverage three years ago they'll probably get it again today.
- Don't shower the media with your press releases. *Always* have something to say because if you keep sending out garbage the very sight of your press release paper will send it into the wastepaper basket.
- Include updated fact sheets on yourself and the team at intervals—don't assume you are so important that journalists will have carefully filed previous ones.

If you don't want the fag of sealing envelopes, keep in mind that agencies exist that will print, collate, and send releases for you (for a fee of course).

Photographs

As far as motorsport is concerned, a photograph is probably worth *more* than a thousand words, particularly for sponsors. In many of the publications you will be trying to reach, photograph standards are not very high and, as with a press release, you will not be trying to create Art. However, do at least try to find a photographer (maybe a friend?) with a little imagination so that you don't appear to have telegraph poles sticking out of your head or are not pictured standing right in front of the sponsor's name on the car. A photograph needs some 'life'—in which context a pretty girl has never done any harm.

Points to keep in mind about photographs:

- Stamps and paper for press releases aren't expensive but the cost of photographs can mount so be a shade selective about where you send them.

- Have 6″ x 8″ black and white as well as colour photographs available—thc use of the latter is growing; television companies will probably prefer colour transparencies.

- Establish who owns the copyright of photographs when commissioning a photographer. (*You* should.) There will be far less chance of photographs being used if publications feel there may be any hassle over copyright.

Finally, don't neglect moving pictures—if, and only if, the quality is high you may get video material used by television companies. If nothing else, the clips may be useful for in-house viewing at sponsors.

Press conferences

If you have a big announcement to make, perhaps about a new team with new cars and new premises, then you may feel it's worth calling a press conference. If so, keep the following in mind:

- Be *sure* you have enough of a story to justify a meeting. Don't wastc people's time if a press release would do just as well.

- Plan, plan, plan, and pay attention to detail (such as having an interpreter available if foreign journalists are present) because the *way* you organize a conference signals as much about you as what is actually said.

- Factory tours can be BORING.

- Take great care over your invitation list. People left out may be offended. Call in friends and colleagues to 'fill' the room if numbers seem likely to be light to avoid people thinking your conference is a flop.

- If television attends expect a fair amount of havoc as they do tend to make a production number out of things, but don't be tempted to treat other journalists as second class.

- Be careful about splashing out on too much booze; it probably won't impress the more erudite journalists. Preferably have coffee available before you speak then wine, etc afterwards.

- Ensure there is NO noise when people are speaking. No 'phones, no extractor fans, no teacups rattling. No noise.

- Be clear who is going to say what and when, who is to introduce them, and so on. *Plant* one or two questions so that there isn't a deathly hush when you call for them. Know when to *stop* answering questions; if you keep dragging them out of journalists you may get one nasty one which will undo much of your earlier good work.

- Give press material out *after* you have made your pitch.
- Have a signing-in book.
- Send material to key people who don't turn up.

Handling interviews

Handling interviews well is an excellent way of promoting yourself. If you are monosyllabic or look disinterested you won't project and you won't get coverage. And what does 'No comment' imply? Yes—something to hide. Because of the importance of interview techniques you may, if funds allow, go on a training course to hone your skills, or if nothing else you may be able to persuade a local journalist to give you a rough ride or two to rehearse your technique. If you have an accent don't go on a course

Client entertaining is a key reason for sponsorship and drivers will often have to 'perform' by talking about a circuit before a race. Here Riccardo Patrese is interviewed by Bob Constandurous at an ICI function.

just to eradicate it; keep it, provided what you say can be understood. And if you learn a foreign language maybe don't become *too* perfect or it may sound less appealing.

Before doing an interview *prepare:* consider the points you want to get across and try to establish why you have been asked, as well as who is doing the interview and how abrasive they are. If on radio or TV, how long will the interview be? If it's a press interview of course the journalist will go on until he has all he needs.

Know your facts. Be on time so that you are not flustered through trying to park; if you are seething either over parking or a race incident, cool down before being interviewed otherwise you may say things you'll regret. Don't drink before an interview; you may become indiscreet and slur your words into the microphone. Don't smoke when being interviewed either.

Don't expect to be told all the questions in advance. You may be, or you may just be given a broad outline before the tape or cameras start. Interviewers on motorsport are unlikely to be hostile, although you may increasingly be asked things like 'How can you justify motorsport with all the environmental concerns?' Worth thinking what you'll say in advance; get a friend to throw such awkward questions at you as practice.

A few other points about interviews:

- *Switch on* and concentrate when doing one. Put some effort into it. If you get known for being good for a quote and a lively interviewee they'll come back to you. Think how scientists—who give the impression that they are slightly unhinged—sometimes become cult figures on television.

- When being interviewed don't constantly moan that you can't get a sponsor, and on no account hold out a begging bowl to the television camera. You will just be seen as a whiner. Put your case for support if appropriate, of course, but do so in a positive way.

- If you've got sponsors, avoid over-long or over-frequent plugs for them. They are *totally* counter-productive.

- Building the questions into your answers may help to get you 'on air' because it will make editing easier.

  Question: Why did you come into the pits on lap 4?
  Answer: I came into the pits on lap 4 because . . .

- *Listen* to the questions. If you don't know the answer, say so. Don't waffle or ramble.

- Admit your mistakes. Mind, if you do you must be prepared for a nature programme to do a feature on you because any driver who does actually admit he made a mistake (instead of blaming the tyres, the car, the track, the phases of the moon, the Martians, or the gearbox) is of course an endangered species.

- Don't use jargon. Curiously enough, the majority of the population find life perfectly possible without a deep understanding of Group A, B, C, etc. If an interviewer is ignorant of such life-enhancing information, *don't* show him up but explain things (briefly).

- Don't pose. Avoid flash jewellery on TV because it will make you look, well . . . flash. Be cautious about using the third person when talking about yourself, as some drivers have been known to do. It sounds faintly absurb when the Royals do it; it will be ridiculous coming from you.

- Don't knock your competition. And although a bit of rivalry can build a good story for the press, be cautious about trying to create or manipulate such 'news' because things may get out of hand.

- You don't *have* to fill any silences. Creating such pauses may be a journalistic technique to make you indiscreet. Be wary too of over-enthusiasm if it is all going swimmingly; you may tell your newfound friend more than you intended.

- As with your mailing list, look for 'stretch' when being interviewed: if it's television, would they like the car in the studio? Would they consider an on-car camera sometime? Keep looking for opportunities. You may even be invited on to one of the junk sport programmes—the events created purely for the box. A driver has even been introduced as a 'star' when his best performance was 17th on a Monte Carlo Rally, so there's hope for you.

Speaking in public

Although the thought of public speaking may make you more nervous than actually competing, you will have to do it sooner or later. Preferably sooner because the more you do, the easier you will find it, although you will never completely conquer nerves. As you climb the ladder you may get invitations to give talks to motor clubs or to speak at their dinner dances; accept these because the standard isn't high for you to be judged against.

Successful speaking comes largely from careful preparation. Start by thinking about your audience. How many will be there? What mix of sexes? How old are they? Why are they there? Above

If you are asked to appear as a 'celebrity' at forums or quizzes then remember you are in showbusiness and try to project a little; don't just grunt and mutter yes or no.

all, what are they expecting from you? A half hour lecture, two sentences to propose a toast, or ... ?

Is it formal or casual dress? What is the start time? Be clear where the venue is and allow plenty of time to get there so that you are not in a panic.

When you have a fairly clear idea of your audience, jot down the points you plan to make in your speech. Put these on cards or slips of paper and then sort them into a logical order so that your speech flows, then build in 'sign posts' to help carry your audience with you, for example: 'That's touring car racing; now, if we look at single-seaters ...'.

Try to find something interesting to say but don't talk in jargon; don't boast, and don't include tedious plugs for sponsors either.

Notes

Having put your points into a logical order, how are you going to remember your speech? Methods vary from memorizing it (which is unnecessarily hard work) to reading it (which is safe but can sound stilted). Perhaps the best compromise is to have a card with a few key bullet points on it to remind you what to say. For instance:

> Second
> First: Small shed
> Magnificent new
> 50–670

could remind you to mention that this is your second visit and that the first time the club met in a shed, now they have this splendid clubhouse and a membership which has shot from 50 to 670, and so on.

Visual aids

When giving lectures or talks (though not after-dinner speeches) you may find visual aids will add impact. If you use charts or slides remember:

- Poor visual aids are worse than none.
- Make them large so that people at the rear can see.
- Have a consistent style.
- Make them honest; don't fake any figures if you are talking to sponsors for instance.

Sponsors may well have the resources to produce visual aids for you, whether they be flipover charts, slides, videos, or whatever Quite apart from the benefit to sponsors, as the anti-motorsport lobby grows through environmentalism (as it is likely to) giving talks to Rotaries, Round Tables, women's groups, and so on is a good way of defending the sport. Overhead projectors can give a nicely relaxed atmosphere because you face the audience and don't need all the lights out. If you need lights out for slides and films, then be sure you sort out in advance who is going to operate the switches.

Rehearsing

Having prepared your notes and, perhaps, visual aids, rehearse enough so that you don't stumble over the words and you have a rough idea of timing, but don't practise so much that you drain all spontaneity from your pitch. If in doubt SHORTEN your speech; audiences never complain if speakers are too brief (you can always fill in with questions) but they do if people drone on too long. Incidentally, when matching words and visual aids leave the latter on view long enough to be understood but don't leave an illustration on display long after you've finished talking about it—if there are stretches of your presentation without specific illustrations then put up a logo or 'wallpaper' instead.

Delivery

On the day, check any final details like the microphone and whether you need to mention a civic dignitary present and then, before you are introduced, be sure the audience is ready to listen to you. If waitresses are still clattering coffee cups or the audience is out of control and throwing bread rolls, then simply refuse to stand up; that's the *organizers'* problem, not yours.

When you do get to your feet SWITCH ON AND CONCENTRATE because you are on stage. Use your natural voice; maintain general eye contact with the audience (don't just transfix one specific person); try to avoid too many extreme gestures, and, last but not least, know when to *stop* talking.

Humour

Note we didn't mention humour when discussing preparation. That's because you do not *have* to use humour when making a speech. Use anecdotes or quotes to lighten your words, but don't string a series of off-colour jokes together and think you've made a speech.

If you do decide to risk humour, and it *is* a risk because you are specifically seeking a reaction, then:

- Avoid 'in' jokes which few of the audience will understand.
- Don't laugh at your own jokes.
- Beware of long complicated jokes—if they've heard them or you get them wrong or tell them badly, the agony is just that more prolonged.

Measuring results

A longer chapter than we expected but the importance of self-promotion cannot be understated in such a marketing driven activity as motorsport.

How will you tell if it has all been worthwhile? By the volume of press clips, by checking whether you met the objectives you wrote down before you started the campaign, and, not least, by the fact that you are simply becoming better known.

A few final points.

- If an interview goes wrong and an article is full of inaccuracies lie down and cool down before reacting.
- Keep any glowing press clips to use in sponsorship presentations.
- Get people to record your radio or TV interviews then play them back and try to learn from any mistakes.

Most important of all, if you do start hitting the headlines through a professional PR approach, don't let it all go to your head—you'll still need to prove you can drive as well as talk if you are to really reach the top.

14

Sponsorship

Because we didn't want to distress you, we have avoided placing undue emphasis on finance so far in this book. But you have to accept that the downside of motorsport is that it is expensive and, unless you have extensive private means or are fortunate enough to find a patron (as old prizefighters did), then sponsorship finding (and keeping) will be an essential part of your make-up as a driver.

Before you seek sponsorship, look in the mirror once again. Be realistic. Why *should* you be sponsored? Would you expect to be sponsored if you took up golf or squash for the first time? Of course not. Why should motorsport be different? Even if you reach

The camaraderie and enjoyment may be greater on, for example, hill climbs (and autotests, sprints, trials et al) than in the 'mainstream' of motorsport.

the giddy heights of running midfield in Formula One, what *real* benefits will sponsors get out of you if, as is likely, the television cameras are following the leading few cars? And if a sponsor won't see much benefit out of Formula One, what is he likely to get out of your efforts in Formula Ford or one of the other lower categories? Not a lot at first sight. However, if a case is properly presented it may still be possible to convince a sponsor of the benefits of supporting you because of local rather than national impact or whatever. But to repeat: be realistic. It won't be easy.

Sponsorship was perhaps the last significant marketing technique to come to the fore and as such, it is less well understood than more 'conventional' techniques like press, TV advertising or poster campaigns. As a result the L.I.F.O. principle may apply and, having been Last In to the marketing mix, sponsorship may be the First Out if budgets get cut in tough times.

However, don't despair. We just point out the facts of life so that you will realize that it is a sellers' market and finding sponsorship is likely to be tough. Before you start looking for sponsorship, consider if you can solve your financial problems in other ways. Do you possess a valuable asset of some sort? Have you considered selling it as an investment in your motorsport future? No? Are you really serious about wanting to get to the top?

Consider what you are seeking sponsorship *for*. Is it so that you can just have a jolly season with your newfound hobby (you won't need us to point out what a thrill *that* approach will give a hard-headed marketing man), or is it to enable you to mount a serious attack on a particular championship?

Having done a little self-appraisal, get organized and treat sponsorship-seeking as a marketing campaign, which is in effect what it will be—almost a military one, in fact. And do allow plenty of time. Marketing departments, at least the intelligent ones, work well ahead and unless you do so too, you will stand little chance of getting on their spending list. Do overcome your natural modesty and promote yourself, as mentioned in the previous chapter, because the better known you are, the better chance you will have of getting sponsorship.

Should you use an agent to help find sponsorship? Probably not in your formative years because you won't be of much benefit to an agent and all he may do (if at all) is prepare a typical brochure and shuffle it around to a few people. Once the first flush of enthusiasm has evaporated you may be forgotten, especially as at this stage you are unlikely to be a 'name'. It may be more productive to seek sponsorship yourself—you may be encouraged to do this if you consider that when marketing directors and managers from the UK's top 300 advertisers were asked in a survey whether they felt sponsorship agencies were generally professional in their approach, the majority thought not. There are extremely good agents around but they are unlikely to want to deal with an unknown like you in your formative years; however, smaller outfits may be able to help you in your campaign by preparing brochures and so on.

If you decide you do want to use an agent, then word of mouth is probably the best way of finding one. Then be quite clear on the terms of payment. Agents may take a percentage based on a sliding scale of, say, 20 per cent up to so much sponsorship funding found, 15 per cent between a higher band and 10 per cent on anything above that. It's up to you to negotiate; obviously, the amount of commission may depend on the amount of work an agent is expected to do.

Are they working exclusively for you or can you in turn use someone else? Who meets their expenses? For general meetings they should, but if you expect them to travel abroad to help you make a presentation it is not unreasonable that they should have their expenses met. Are there any sponsors you are not prepared to

If you have several sponsors, resolve who has what and where on the car before the first event. Some negotiation and diplomacy may be necessary to placate everyone.

take for ethical, moral, or religious reasons? If so, spell these out at the start and do bear in mind that the more restrictive you are the more you reduce your chances. Your biggest conscience clash may be over tobacco sponsorship, with your high principles becoming eroded as your cash crisis deepens. Nevertheless, avoid tobacco funding if you can because it may reduce your media exposure in some markets because of local laws.

Don't appoint an agent and then forget him, expecting a miraculous cheque to appear in due course: unless you maintain contact you will be forgotten and won't get sponsorship.

Whether or not you have an agent, spend time analysing what you have to offer potential sponsors and then consider how to present it in the best way. List the various benefits you are offering, such as the sponsor's name on the car and support vehicles, decals on overalls, opportunities for client entertaining, and so on. And on—the opportunities are almost endless. Entertaining key customers at events is a major area of sponsorship, although, for obvious reasons, it tends to be less effective on rallies than at race tracks; but when offering tickets be careful that your sponsor isn't a major business rival of the sponsors of a meeting. It may not matter, but at least make them aware of a possible clash.

You may be able to offer banners at events and free ads in programmes, although these may be beyond your gift because they are controlled by event organizers. Perhaps you can offer space for product displays by your transporter if nowhere else. Or there may be opportunities for selling team clothing (with the sponsor's name and logo on of course).

Above all, offer visits to test sessions because one of the key advantages of sponsorship over most other marketing techniques is that it offers sponsors 'what can't be bought'. A visit to a rehearsal of a ballet or play is often a heck of a lot more interesting than going to the event itself; a peek behind the scenes of motorsport can be equally compelling.

Mention the media coverage a link with you will generate and highlight any likely TV coverage of the events. It's perhaps not as important as the TV companies think (or even as important as people claim when making sponsorship approaches), but nevertheless if you know there will be guaranteed TV coverage then make that a key plank in your sponsorship platform. Mention, too, if radio stations will be covering the events and whether the press will be specifically interested. If they gave extensive coverage in previous years to the same events, then include a press montage to show the likely exposure this time. Similarly, include any attendance or market research figures to

Modern marketing men may imply that they personally invented advertising and sponsorship; note the banners on this event in 1924.

support your case.

Your particular list of sponsorship benefits may include: the driver being available for in-house talks with the car on display to help motivate employees (hence the earlier emphasis on public speaking); in-store promotions as well as visits to schools if, say, the sponsors are aiming at the youth market. You could perhaps add that motorsport does not suffer from the amateur versus professional squabble which affect other sports, nor does it have any drug scandals.

In drawing up a list of things you can offer, *don't promise what you can't deliver.* If you do, you may con a sponsor one year, but you certainly won't keep him the next. He may well be turned off motorsport sponsorship for a long time and, worse, he will almost certainly tell his business friends. Sponsorship is not charity or patronage; it is—or should be—a two-way business agreement with you giving something of value and receiving money in return.

Should you quote a price when making an initial sponsorship approach? Yes, if the figure is relatively small. If it is large then maybe put 'we can discuss at a meeting'. Bear in mind when quoting figures that you can always negotiate downwards but you will never be able to negotiate upwards, so if you go in too low you may lose out. How should you fix a price? Well, traditionally people charge or try to charge what they need which, if you think about it, is the wrong approach. You should charge *what the market will stand.* If you are doing a low category championship but want to build a new workshop and quote a sponsorship figure with this in mind, then it will be unrealistically high and poor value. On the other hand, if a championship you are doing gets local TV coverage then you can ask more than if it was just being covered by a local freesheet.

Liaise with other drivers and teams and try to get a feel for what sort of revenue they are getting so that you do not undercut the market or, conversely, aim for a hopelessly unrealistic sum. Try to relate the cost to 'something'—so many insertions of an ad in the local paper, or whatever. Incidentally, if you find haggling is distressing then this is one area where you may decide to use an agent, although if you are not tough enough to conduct negotiations perhaps you should find a more gentle pastime.

Having analysed what you've got to offer and considered a price for it, you now have to present your package. Most sponsors or potential sponsors prefer a brief letter with some form of backup; the style of the backup depends on what you are seeking because to some extent the documentation should reflect this. If it's over-ornate and too lavish you may impress some sponsors but the majority may think you are wasting your money on unnecessary frills when you could be spending it on parts for your car. On the other hand you are unlikely to raise millions for F1 with a duplicated and smudged letter with spelling mistakes.

When you've prepared a letter and/or brochure setting out your proposal, it may be worth getting it vetted by a hard-nosed businessman, someone used to receiving such material. Get him to play devil's advocate, too, in asking searching and awkward questions about what you are offering.

So you're all ready. You've thought everything out. You've got a well-crafted letter and an exciting brochure. So the sponsorship money will roll in, won't it? No, it won't because thousands of other people will have done exactly the same; they will have similar letters, similar brochures, similar hopes. And don't forget people in *other* sports will be searching for money too. So, before you start sending off letters and brochures, consider *who you know.* Strings are meant to be pulled, so pull them.

If that route fails and you have to start mailing letters and brochures, do be realistic. Consider whether your approach should be national or local; if you are a youngster at a relatively early stage in your career, then a local sponsor is much more likely to come on board than a national one. Draw up a list of companies to approach and don't neglect unusual possibilities—some sponsorship links get extra media mileage simply because they

Don't just go for the obvious people when seeking sponsorship. Drinks companies don't appear very logical links — until handled like this.

are, at first sight, unusual. Don't restrict your approaches to the 'conventional' motorsport sponsors who get countless appeals as it is.

Consider other unorthodox approaches—perhaps 'space to let' signs on your competition car. However, don't let such things become too plaintive or they will be counterproductive—just as if you keep moaning 'I can't find a sponsor', then you will simply be seen as a whiner . . . and a loser.

Plan your approach. Keep copies of letters as well as a log of any sent and received. Address correspondence to the right people; it's not absolutely vital that you address a letter to the marketing director by name but it won't do any harm and it will show you've made an effort.

Put at the end of a letter something along the lines of 'I will call you in a few days to discuss.' Now this may simply alert the recipient to tell his secretary to say that he is out when you call, but you may still get a few successes by this route. If you've said you'll call, then *do* so.

Keep in mind that if you send out a hundred letters, ten people may reply, of which two may be mildly interested. Don't be too disheartened by this response rate—it's not you, it's the way things work because, incredibly, even major companies don't bother to reply to sponsorship requests. Why? Because they get so many of them. We did warn you it would be tough.

Few sponsors are likely to commit to sponsor you without a face to face meeting, and in fact the main aim in sending out mailshots or making 'phone calls should be to arrange such meetings.

The key to successful presentation and negotiation at a meeting is preparation. Brief yourself beforehand on the company, its products, and its policies. Has it sponsored other areas? Do you know people in those areas? If so, find out how successful the links were and if any snags were encountered because the company is likely to raise queries on these things with you. Forewarned will be forearmed.

Consider how you are going to reply if the sponsor says he doesn't like the idea of being linked with a dangerous sport. There is no evidence that any odium attaches to a sponsor if his name is on the side of a car that crashes, but it does bother some companies so think what your response will be. And think, too, how you will handle queries about the apparent clash between motorsport and environmental concerns. You also need to brace yourself for questions on your likely success rate because sponsors do like winners, even though there is no real evidence that a car has to win to benefit a sponsor if it is still getting media coverage and the link is being properly promoted.

Decide who is to make the presentation at a meeting with a sponsor. Sponsors may not be impressed by being hopelessly outnumbered so don't go mob handed, and if there's a particularly abrasive character in your team it may be wise to leave him at home; the life and soul of the team may simply get up sponsors' noses. Rehearse what you are going to say and consider whether any visual aids will reinforce your case—as they should in such a glamorous and exciting activity as motorsport. Simple flip-over charts neatly prepared may help your presentation, as of course may a video; in fact people are now preparing videos specifically extolling their talents to help get sponsorship. These may be fine when shown in a meeting but don't be so sure that people will bother to watch them if you simply mail them.

If you plan to use a video, slides, or other visual aids, do have the right equipment available and try to gain access to the meeting room in advance so that you can make sure everything works; you won't impress a potential sponsor if you dwell on the hi-tech image of motorsport then can't find the plug for the projector.

Arrive in good time for a meeting and when it gets underway *don't ramble*. You must find out in advance how long the potential sponsor is likely to have and if, say, you have half an hour you should plan no more than ten minutes for your pitch to allow plenty of time for discussion. You may need to set the scene by explaining what your particular area of motorsport is all about; one of the most off-putting times for someone making a presentation is when the potential sponsor's eyes glaze over at the complexity of it all. Oh, how motorsport needs to simplify itself.

It will be even more off-putting if hints are made about 'backhanders' should a sponsor come on board. We strongly recommend avoiding such deals at all costs but you need to be worldly enough to know that they happen; with the high cost of motorsport it's not surprising that more falls off the back of moral lorries than in other sports. If you graduate to the international scene, the question of tax may arise and the line between evasion and avoidance may become decidedly fine. Care!

Don't expect quick decisions from sponsors, and don't be over-optimistic. A friendly farewell and a promise to 'think about it' is likely to indicate no more than that the marketing man is a kind bloke and is letting you down as gently as possible. You may never hear from him again.

Send a polite 'thank you for seeing us' letter after a meeting and if any queries were raised, answer them. In other words, use the letter to reinforce your case.

You will probably have to juggle negotiations with several sponsors at once because companies may take weeks to make decisions so you will need more than one approach on the boil at any time. You just need a disciplined approach to your campaign. If you hector a potential sponsor with 'if I don't hear by Friday, I'm offering it to someone else', just one thing is certain: you won't hear by Friday.

Keeping a sponsor

If you eventually find a sponsor, don't bank his cheque, heave a sigh of relief, and then do nothing else. If you take this approach you won't keep the sponsor in future years.

The key to retaining a sponsor at the *end* of a project is what happens at the *start* of a link. Both parties must know exactly what the conditions are and these should be put in writing. It doesn't necessarily need to be a legal contract; in fact if you get too many lawyers involved you will probably find the season is over before you actually exchange contracts. But there should at least be an exchange of letters spelling out who does what, what is expected of each side, and above all 'what happens if it rains?' In other words, what happens if things go awry and, for example, the team does nine races instead of the stipulated ten? What happens if a driver breaks an arm and can't race? What happens if banners can't be put up as promised? Etc. etc. Think about such calamities in advance, so that if something happens at least people know exactly where they stand.

The contract or exchange of letters should spell out how you should be paid. There is a case for receiving, say, one-third of the sponsorship fee upfront simply for being involved, with the other two-thirds split on a per event basis; if one event is then not done the sponsor knows how much he is due to be refunded. It doesn't really matter what the system is provided both sides are happy with it and it is written down, repeat *written down*. If it isn't, a key person in the sponsoring company may leave and his successor may not accept your word about what his predecessor promised. With large companies it may be wise to plead to be put on their 'fast track' for payments.

During the season do all you can to *involve* the sponsor. Ideally, you should encourage the sponsor to have one person as your liaison man so that you don't have to keep fighting your way through company channels. If more than one sponsor is involved then encourage them to have regular liaison meetings to explore how to get the maximum stretch from the sponsorship.

Whoever your sponsor/s you must work hard to present a professional line-up like this.

A key area will of course be media liaison. Take a little care to understand the sponsor's policy towards the media because if you blunder in (trying to be helpful) you may simply fall foul of their careful procedures. But do, where possible, put ideas to the sponsor to extend the media coverage. In seeking new ideas, don't neglect the tried and tested old ones. We know from experience that if you do a 'production line' exercise with sponsors' guests photographed one by one alongside a competition car and driver, and the photographs are then sent to the guests' local newspapers (with their permission of course) then a very high percentage will be printed. Easy? Cheap? Of course. So why do so few sponsors make the effort? Encourage yours to do so.

Keep your word, involve your sponsor, and if things start to go wrong (and sadly they sometimes do) then get together with the sponsor at an early stage *before* relationships have broken down completely.

Well, here endeth the lesson. We hope this book will help you to make it to the top in motorsport. In won't be easy but you can do it if you work at it. We wish you luck but remember: the harder you work the luckier you will be.

Appendix A

Find-a-Driver Questionnaire

While the authors would not claim that it is possible to readily find a star driver through psychological testing, the following questionnaire has proved effective in broadbrush assessment programmes throughout Europe. You may care to take a stab at the questions *before* reading the marking on the next page. Questions 1 to 10—not shown—asked about height, weight, whether people smoked, etc.

Questions

Please read each of the following statements and circle the answer which applies to you. Base your answers on experience you have already gained from sport (of any kind).

SA If you strongly agree with it.
A If you agree with it.
U If you are uncertain.
D If you disagree with it.
SD If you strongly disagree with it.

eg.	A good car is important for success in motorsport.	(SA) A U D SD
11	In a sporting event I feel more confident than the other competitors.	SA A U D SD
12	Competing is more important than winning.	SA A U D SD
13	Confidence is more important than motivation.	SA A U D SD
14	Natural talent is the most important quality for success.	SA A U D SD
15	I never doubt my sporting ability.	SA A U D SD
16	A poor start usually means a poor result.	SA A U D SD
17	Instant reaction to problems is more important than prior planning.	SA A U D SD
18	An hour before an event I would be rather nervous.	SA A U D SD
19	Anxiety is necessary for good performance	SA A U D SD
20	I would be nervous during a Motorsport event.	SA A U D SD
21	Thinking about mistakes during a competition improves my performance.	SA A U D SD
22	Good performance is more important than winning.	SA A U D SD
23	Success is due more to flair than to industry.	SA A U D SD
24	Innate ability is more important than determination.	SA A U D SD

25	Concentration is more important than intelligence.	SA A U D SD
26	Prior preparation is the most important ingredient for success.	SA A U D SD
27	Someone should watch me drive and discuss my performance with me.	SA A U D SD
28	It is wise to take advice on competition driving from a number of people	SA A U D SD
29	Too much advice would leave me confused	SA A U D SD
30	Health worries never concern me.	SA A U D SD

Marking Key

Question No.	SA	A	U	D	SD
11	2	3	1	5	4
12	2	5	1	4	3
13	1	2	3	5	4
14	4	5	1	3	2
15	2	3	0	4	5
16	1	2	2	4	5
17	2	5	1	4	3
18	4	5	1	3	2
19	4	5	1	3	2
20	1	2	3	4	5
21	1	2	3	5	4
22	4	5	1	3	2
23	1	2	3	4	5
24	3	4	1	5	2
25	2	3	1	5	4
26	5	4	1	3	2
27	5	4	3	2	1
28	4	5	1	3	2
29	2	3	1	4	5
30	2	3	1	5	4

Note: A score of 83 and above means that you have a reasonable profile but of course you still need ability. Don't despair if your score is lower—you may be the exception which proves the rule. Obviously such a test *cannot* tell whether you can drive a car well—what experience suggests it *can* do is tell whether you have a logical and organized mind which will help you withstand the inevitable pressures of motorsport. During Find-a-Driver appraisals, the authors have found that those with the higher marks are able to cope better with unexpected spins and the like.

Appendix B

First Aid

Motorsport is dangerous and as a competitor you are more likely to come across an accident than the average motorist. Therefore find time to learn a bit about first aid. If possible watch a video on the subject and go on a training course—think what an incompetent fool you'd feel if you had to stand by helpless at a serious accident.

The following advice is not intended to be exhaustive—just a brief guide to what to do at an accident. If there are marshals or police present then obey their instructions—don't add to the likely confusion by simply barging in. If there are no officials at the scene then:

- Protect the scene of the accident—send someone up the road to alert other cars so that they slow or stop. If you don't do this a simple accident can become a multiple one.

- Switch off ignitions and stop people smoking—this should be obvious but people with frayed nerves may light up.

- Check the breathing of any casualties not able to speak. If someone is NOT breathing, tilt their head back, pinch their nose shut, and blow air into their lungs—their chest should rise. Remove your mouth, let air out; repeat every five seconds until breathing restarts. (This is mouth to mouth resuscitation and is one of the most important things to learn; try to see a practical demonstration some time; it's not as difficult or unpleasant or as complicated as it sounds).

- If someone is bleeding badly, *press* on the bleeding area firmly with your fingers, thumb, and hand; if help is available, replace with dry dressing and a firm bandage. Ensure that bleeding stops—if not, revert to hand pressure.

- Don't move a casualty from a car unless there is real danger from, say, fire or drowning, because they may have a fractured spine. Wait for skilled help otherwise you may make their injuries much worse.

- Unconscious casualties outside a vehicle should be placed in the 'three-quarter prone position', ie almost face down. Make sure they are breathing easily—DO NOT LEAVE them until they regain consciousness.
- Send someone to get skilled help—ambulance, rescue vehicle, etc.

The best advice is DON'T PANIC. It may not be easy, particularly if there is blood about, but if you keep calm while everyone else is flapping, you really may save someone's life.

Appendix C

Rental Agreement Terms and Conditions

THIS RENTAL AGREEMENT is made the   day of   19....
BETWEEN   A PREPARATION COMPANY LIMITED registered office One
Industrial Unit, Anytown (hereinafter called 'the Lessor') of the
one part and
A DRIVER.
of Two Main Street, Othertown
(hereinafter called 'the Renter') of the othcr part
WHEREAS
(1) The Lessor agrees to rent and hereby does rent to the Renter
the vehicle described in the 1st Schedule annexed hereto
(hereinafter called 'the vehicle') subject to all the terms and
conditions contained herein
(2) The Lessor agrees to perform the duties and honour the
obligations set out in the 2nd Schedule hereto
(3) The Renter agrees to perform the duties and honour the
obligations set out in the 3rd Schedule hereto
(4)   The Renter hereby acknowledges and it is agreed as
hereinafter appears:
1.   That the Renter will return the vehicle together with all
wheels tyres spares car documents accessories and equipment to
the Lessor or its duly authorized servants or agents at the end of
each rally as specified in the 4th Schedule hereto
2.   That the vehicle shall not be operated:
  a)   To transfer goods in violation of Customs regulations or in
      any other illegal manner
  b)   To carry passengers or property for a consideration express
      or implied
  c)   To propel or tow any trailer without the consent of the
      Lessor

d) In motorsport events other than those specified in the 4th Schedule hereto

e) By any person driving when unfit through drink or drugs

f) By any person other than

    (i) The Renter or any person(s) nominated or employed by the Renter who is approved in writing by the Lessor and who is duly qualified and holds a current valid driving licence

    (ii) In case of breakdown or accident a motor vehicle repairer provided he is duly qualified and licensed

g) Outside Spain without the express consent of the Lessor

3. That the Renter is personally liable to pay to the Lessor on demand:

a) The sum of £x sterling (amount in words) (hereinafter called 'the initial payment') being 25 per cent of the total hire charge. Such sum to be deposited in the Lessor's Bank no later than 3 February 19....

b) The sum of £y sterling (amount in words) to be deposited in the Lessor's Bank not later than 7 days prior to the start of each rally specified in the 4th Schedule

c) The sum of £z sterling (amount in words) to be deposited in the Lessors's Bank by the 29 January 19 . . . in respect of the Lessor painting the vehicle to a scheme supplied by the Renter such scheme to be received by the Lessor not later than 29 January 19 . . .

d) All fines and court costs for parking traffic or other legal violations assessed against the vehicle, Renter, other drivers, or Lessor until the vehicle is returned to the possession of the Lessor except where caused through the fault of the Lessor

e) Lessor's costs including reasonable legal fees where permitted by law incurred collecting any payments due from the Renter hereunder

f) Value Added Tax and all other taxes (if any) payable on the aforesaid items

g) The Lessor's legal costs incurred in the preparation of this Agreement

4. The Renter shall provide his own insurance for the vehicles as follows:-

a) Insure the vehicle specified in the 1st Schedule against all third party risks whatsoever and against damage or loss by fire or theft to a value of not less than £30,000.00 sterling (Thirty thousand pounds sterling) and produce to the Lessor a valid certificate of such insurance no later than 7 days before the 1st Rally specified in the 4th Schedule

b) Maintain such insurance cover throughout the duration of

this Agreement and in relation to each and every one of the rallies specified in the 4th Schedule and ensure that the Lessor's name is endorsed on the policy as the owner of the vehicle

c) Insure the body shell of the vehicle for each and every rally specified in the 4th Schedule to a minimum insured value of £6000 sterling (Six thousand pounds sterling) and produce a valid certificate of such insurance to the Lessor not less than 7 days before each rally

d) All such insurances as aforesaid shall be entered into with a first class insurance company to be approved in writing by the Lessor on completion of this Agreement or as subsequently approved by the Lessor from time to time at its absolute discretion

e) Comply with the terms and conditions of the Insurance Policy and pay to the Lessor any excess in the event of a claim

f) (i) In the event of the insurers withholding or refusing indemnity to indemnify the Lessor in respect of any loss or damage to the vehicle and all claims from third parties which may arise

 (ii) To provide the Lessor with a bond in support of such indemnity in the sum of £30,000 sterling (Thirty thousand pounds sterling) guaranteed by the Renter's Bank such Bond to be approved by the Lessor. Such Bond to remain in force throughout the entire period of rental and evidence thereof to be produce to the Lessor not later than 7 days before the 1st rally specified in the 4th Schedule

g) If any claim is made against the insurers allow the Lessor to conduct any negotiation and effect any settlement with Insurers and agree to abide by any settlement or arrangement with the insurers by the Lessor. Any monies payable by the Insurers shall be paid to the Lessor as the Lessor shall direct.

5. That the Renter hereby releases and indemnifies the Lessor from and against any liability for loss or damage to any property (including costs relating thereto) left stored or transported by the Renter or any other person in or upon the vehicle before or after return of the vehicle to the Lessor its servants or agents

6. That the Lessor whilst taking all precautions and using its best efforts to prevent such happening shall not be liable for any loss or damage arising from any fault or defects in or from mechanical failure of the vehicle or any consequential loss or damage

7. In the event of any breach by the Renter of any of the terms and conditions hereof the Lessor may without notice terminate this agreement and if the vehicle is in the possession of the Renter may without notice repossess the vehicles and for such

purpose may enter upon premises where the vehicle may be and remove the same and the Renter shall be responsible for and indemnify the Lessor against all actions costs and damages consequent upon or arising from such repossession and removal

8. Any alteration or addition to these terms shall be null and void unless agreed upon in writing by the parties

9. That this agreement shall be governed by and construed in accordance with the Laws of England and Wales and that the English version hereof shall be the definitive version

10. If the Renter shall not compete in all the rallies specified in the 4th Schedule the Initial Payment shall be forfeited and will become the absolute property of the Lessor

THE 1st SCHEDULE

1. The vehicle: FORD SIERRA COSWORTH registration No ABC 123
2. The Specification: To comply with the FISA "Group N" regulations and so far as possible the Lessor shall ensure that the vehicle is prepared to the Lessor's most up to date specification from time to time, within that category. The vehicle will be left hand drive.

THE 2nd SCHEDULE

The Lessor's Obligations

1. The Lessor will prepare and re-prepare the vehicle in a good and workmanlike manner for each rally specified in the 4th Schedule

2. After each such rally the Lessor may replace such parts of the vehicle as may be, in the Lessor's absolute discretion, necessary

3. The Lessor will provide, for each rally specified in the 4th Schedule, one service vehicle complete with such spares as the Lessor shall deem sufficient for on-rally use together with two rally engineers.

4. The Lessor shall pay and be responsible for all bookings of ferries hotels and fuel for the service vehicle, rally car and two rally engineers in respect of their travel to and from each rally specified in the 4th Schedule

5. The Lessor shall prepare, in respect of each rally aforesaid, a movement schedule prior to each said rally, a copy of which will be supplied to the Renter his servants or agents

6. The Lessor will replace major parts and components from time to time as it in its absolute discretion deems necessary

7. The Lessor will provide 20 wheels for the Renter's use with the vehicle at each said rally event such wheels to be returned to

the Lessor by the Renter after each said rally

The Renter shall be liable for all damage and/or costs occasioned to the said wheels during each said rally notwithstanding how such damage may have been caused

THE 3rd SCHEDULE

The Renter's Obligations

1. To pay all demands and sums as aforesaid and to honour all its obligations and comply with the terms of this Agreement

2. To pay all hotel bills including breakfast, for the rally engineers supplied by the Lessor on each specified rally and to pay for all fuel used on each rally aforesaid by the service vehicle also supplied by the Lessor

3. In respect of each rally specified in the 4th Schedule to provide to the Lessor not less than 14 days before each said rally the date, time and place of the start and finish of that rally and the address telephone number and booking details of the hotel(s) which the Renter has booked for the said rally in order to comply with his obligations under (2) above

4. To pay all road-tolls, fuel consumption of the vehicle, and for all rally wheels and tyres used on each specified rally except only as referred to in Paragraph 7 of the 2nd Schedule

5. To pay for all damage occasioned to the vehicle whilst being driven by the Renter or whilst under his care or control. Such damage to be repaired by the Lessor at the rate of £12.00 sterling (twelve pounds sterling) per hour for labour and replacement parts at recommended retail price

6. To supply to the Lessor free of charge before the first specified rally the following parts to be fitted by the Lessor to the vehicle

MONROE FRONT STRUTS: 300/110 rate

MONROE REAR SHOCK ABSORBERS: 240/110 rate

THE 4th SCHEDULE

The Specified Rallies:

SIGNED by the Lessor:

SIGNED by the Renter:

Index